Dor

DOREEN FULLEYLOV... name of Ruth Morgan... career she travelled ex... viewing readers and... She has always loved the country, especially... she lived for many years in a 17th-century farmhouse with her husband, a mushroom grower, and her children.

Country Fare

Doreen Fulleylove

Hamlyn Paperbacks

First published 1970 by
The Hamlyn Publishing Group Ltd,
as *Simple Country Fare*
Hamlyn Paperbacks edition 1979
Third printing 1982
Copyright © 1970 by
The Hamlyn Publishing Group Ltd.

ISBN 0 600 38394 6

Hamlyn Paperbacks are published by
The Hamlyn Publishing Group Ltd,
Astronaut House, Hounslow Road,
Feltham, Middlesex TW14 9AR

Made and printed in Great Britain by
Hazell Watson & Viney Ltd, Aylesbury, Bucks

Line drawings by Richard Osborne

CONTENTS

Useful Facts and Figures

Notes on metrication

In this book quantities are given in metric and Imperial measures. Exact conversion from Imperial to metric measures does not usually give very convenient working quantities and so the metric measures have been rounded off into units of 25 grams. The table below shows the recommended equivalents.

Ounces	Approx g to nearest whole figure	Recommended conversion to nearest unit of 25
1	28	25
2	57	50
3	85	75
4	113	100
5	142	150
6	170	175
7	198	200
8	227	225
9	255	250
10	283	275
11	312	300
12	340	350
13	368	375
14	396	400
15	425	425
16 (1 lb)	454	450
17	482	475
18	510	500
19	539	550
20 (1¼ lb)	567	575

Note When converting quantities over 20 oz first add the appropriate figures in the centre column, then adjust to the nearest unit of 25. As a general guide, 1 kg (1000 g) equals 2·2 lb or about 2 lb 3 oz. This method of conversion gives good results in nearly all cases, although in certain pastry and cake recipes a more accurate conversion is necessary to produce a balanced recipe.

Liquid measures The millilitre has been used in this book and the following table gives a few examples.

Imperial	Approx ml to nearest whole figure	Recommended ml
$\frac{1}{4}$ pint	142	150 ml
$\frac{1}{2}$ pint	283	300 ml
$\frac{3}{4}$ pint	425	450 ml
1 pint	567	600 ml
$1\frac{1}{2}$ pints	851	900 ml
$1\frac{3}{4}$ pints	992	1000 ml (1 litre)

Spoon measures All spoon measures given in this book are level unless otherwise stated.

Can sizes At present, cans are marked with the exact (usually to the nearest whole number) metric equivalent of the Imperial weight of the contents, so we have followed this practice when giving can sizes.

Oven temperatures

The table below gives recommended equivalents. It is an approximate guide only. Different makes of cooker vary and if you are in any doubt about the setting it is as well to refer to the manufacturer's temperature chart.

	°C	°F	Gas Mark
Very cool	110	225	$\frac{1}{4}$
	120	250	$\frac{1}{2}$
Cool	140	275	1
	150	300	2
Moderate	160	325	3
	180	350	4
Moderately hot	190	375	5
	200	400	6
Hot	220	425	7
	230	450	8
Very hot	240	475	9

Notes for American and Australian users

In America the 8-oz measuring cup is used. In Australia metric measures are now used in conjunction with the standard 250-ml measuring cup. The Imperial pint, used in Britain and Australia, is 20 fl oz, while the American pint is 16 fl oz. It is important to remember that the Australian tablespoon differs from both the British and American tablespoons; the table below gives a comparison. The British standard tablespoon, which has been used through this book, holds 17·7 ml, the American 14·2 ml, and the Australian 20 ml. A teaspoon holds approximately 5 ml in all three countries.

British	American	Australian
1 teaspoon	1 teaspoon	1 teaspoon
1 tablespoon	1 tablespoon	1 tablespoon
2 tablespoons	3 tablespoons	2 tablespoons
3½ tablespoons	4 tablespoons	3 tablespoons
4 tablespoons	5 tablespoons	3½ tablespoons

An Imperial/American guide to solid and liquid measures

Solid measures

IMPERIAL	AMERICAN
1 lb butter or margarine	2 cups
1 lb flour	4 cups
1 lb granulated or castor sugar	2 cups
1 lb icing sugar	3 cups
8 oz rice	1 cup

Liquid measures

IMPERIAL	AMERICAN
¼ pint liquid	⅔ cup liquid
½ pint	1¼ cups
¾ pint	2 cups
1 pint	2½ cups
1½ pints	3¾ cups
2 pints	5 cups (2½ pints)

Note When making any of the recipes in this book, only follow one set of measures as they are not interchangeable.

Introduction

There is great pleasure and satisfaction in cooking traditional country fare, using the bountiful raw material available in our farms, gardens and orchards.

For more years than I care to remember I have been a cookery writer for national magazines. In the course of my work I have travelled all over the country meeting housewives and collecting their recipes and cookery ideas. Whether in a remote Scottish croft, Welsh hill farm or on a modern housing estate I have everywhere met pride in the craft of cooking and a long tradition of know-how stretching back through daughter and mother to the days of our rural forefathers.

The purpose of this book is to record some of the great recipes that have delighted our forebears, including as well some contributions from the modern country housewife.

The big farm kitchen where I am working probably hasn't changed much since the time of Charles II and Samuel Pepys. The beams are dark, the great open fireplace is blackened by the smoke of centuries of fires and the Kentish hills still make the same lovely picture through the leaded lights of the windows.

For centuries in this room appetites have been appeased, festivals celebrated, marriages cheered, christenings made merry and the rigours of farming comforted by the good fare prepared here. Now it is my family, children and grandchildren who gather here for all family occasions. Perhaps the friendly ghosts of my predecessors have secretly encouraged me to write this book.

Around Britain Recipes

The astonishing thing about our small country is its infinite variety. Variety of scenery, of people, of culture, of dialect. And so with regional dishes – traditional recipes which are well worth preserving amidst the uniformity of modern life.

The very names of these dishes capture the feeling of broad acres and sturdy appetites. Here are just a few: Chipstead churdles, Shropshire fitchett pie, Hereford one-pot mince, Wiltshire porkies, Sussex pond pudding, Irish soda bread, Bara brith, Lincolnshire plum bread, Fen Country sweet potato cake. And many, many more. Most are simple to make, all are good to eat.

Savoury Recipes

YORKSHIRE BACON AND EGG PIE

Cooking time   about 1 hour
Oven temperature   Moderately hot
200°C, 400°F, Gas Mark 6 for 30 minutes;
moderate 180°C, 350°F, Gas Mark 4 for 25–30 minutes
Serves 4

METRIC/IMPERIAL

275 g/10 oz short crust pastry (see page 69)	salt and pepper
for filling	225 g/8 oz lean bacon
2 tomatoes, sliced	4 medium eggs
1 tablespoon grated onion	*for glaze*
	beaten egg

Roll out half the pastry into a round and use to line a 20-cm/8-inch ovenproof pie plate. Trim edges with a knife. Arrange slices of tomato to cover the base. Top with grated onion and seasoning. Trim rind from bacon rashers, chop into small pieces with a knife. Place bacon on top of tomato and onion, leaving four hollows. Carefully break a whole egg into each hollow. Season lightly. Damp edges and place pastry lid in position. Lightly press together and trim away excess pastry. Knock up and flute edges with back of knife. Cut diamond shapes from trimmings and use to decorate pie. Glaze with beaten egg.

Bake on shelf above the centre in a moderately hot oven for 30 minutes. Reduce heat to moderate for further 25–30 minutes, or until pastry and filling are cooked through. Serve hot with vegetables or cold with salad.

BUCKINGHAMSHIRE DUMPLING

Cooking time   2½ hours
Serves 4

METRIC/IMPERIAL

450 g/1 lb self-raising flour	2 large onions, finely chopped
1 teaspoon salt	1 tablespoon dried sage
175 g/6 oz shredded suet	salt and pepper
300 ml/½ pint cold water	*to serve*
225 g/8 oz bacon, chopped	brown gravy
225 g/8 oz liver, chopped	

Sift flour and salt, add suet and mix to a stiff dough with water; roll out on a floured board to a strip 18 by 45 cm/7 by 18 inches long. Cover dough with chopped bacon, liver, onions, sage and seasoning. Roll up tightly and wrap in well-greased foil. Steam for about 2½ hours. Remove foil and serve with brown gravy.

WILTSHIRE PORKIES

Cooking time   20 minutes
Serves 4

METRIC/IMPERIAL

110 g/4 oz plain flour	450 g/1 lb sausage meat
½ teaspoon salt	2 apples, peeled, cored and cut
1 egg	into rings
1 tablespoon cooking oil	*for frying*
about 150 ml/¼ pint water	deep fat

Mix flour and salt in a basin. Separate the egg and add egg yolk, oil and enough water to make a batter which will coat the back of a spoon. With floured hands form sausage meat into small neat rolls. Whisk egg white stiffly and fold into the batter. Coat each roll with batter and fry in deep hot fat for 10–15 minutes until golden brown.
Drain on kitchen paper. Pile on serving dish.

Coat apple rings in remaining batter and deep fry for 5 minutes, drain, then arrange round the 'porkies'.

WILTSHIRE FRUITY PORK HOT-POT

Cooking time   2 hours
Oven temperature   Moderately hot
190°C, 375°F, Gas Mark 5
Serves 4

METRIC/IMPERIAL

4 pork chops	4 tomatoes
1 pig's kidney	225 g/8 oz onions
1 tablespoon seasoned flour	450–675 g/1–1½ lb potatoes
½ teaspoon mixed herbs	450 ml/¾ pint perry
1 medium cooking apple	

Trim the meat and kidney, and cut kidney into neat pieces. Mix the seasoned flour and herbs and use to coat the meats. Peel, core and slice the apple, skin tomatoes, leaving them whole. Peel onions and potatoes, then cut into thin slices.

Put into a large casserole or hot-pot dish half the potatoes, half the onions and half the apple. Add the chops, kidney and the tomatoes. Cover with remaining apple, onions and potatoes, in that order. Sprinkle any remaining seasoned flour on top, and add extra seasonings to taste. Pour in the perry and cover with lid.

Cook in moderately hot oven for 2 hours, removing the lid for the last 15 minutes.

HEREFORD ONE-POT MINCE

Cooking time   about 1 hour
Serves 4

METRIC/IMPERIAL

450 g/1 lb minced beef	4 small onions
40 g/1½ oz dripping	4 tomatoes
25 g/1 oz plain flour	8–12 small potatoes
salt and pepper	*for garnish*
450 ml/¾ pint cider	chopped parsley

Fry the mince in a little dripping in a saucepan until well browned, stirring constantly with a fork. Sprinkle the flour over the meat and mix in with salt and pepper. Add the cider and simmer for 5 minutes, stirring.

Peel the onions, tomatoes and potatoes and place, whole, in a pan or casserole. Pour in the mince and cover with a lid. Simmer for about 40 minutes until vegetables are cooked. Arrange vegetables round edge of a serving dish and pour mince into centre. Garnish with chopped parsley.

LANCASHIRE HOT-POT

Cooking time   2½–3 hours
Oven temperature   Moderate
160°C, 325°F, Gas Mark 3
Serves 4

METRIC/IMPERIAL

675 g/1½ lb middle neck mutton	2 large onions
2 sheep's kidneys (optional)	salt and pepper
450–675 g/1–1½ lb potatoes	300 ml/½ pt stock

Trim the meat and kidneys and cut into neat pieces. Peel the potatoes thinly and slice. Slice the onions thinly. Put layers of the meat and vegetables into a greased casserole. Season each layer well and finish with a layer of potatoes. Add about 300 ml/½ pint stock or water and cover with casserole lid or aluminium foil.

Bake in a moderate oven for about 2½–3 hours, removing the lid for the last 30 minutes to brown the potatoes. Add small dabs of dripping or butter if potatoes get too dry during cooking.

CHIPSTEAD CHURDLES

Cooking time   about 45 minutes
Oven temperature   Moderately hot
190°C, 375°F, Gas Mark 5
Makes 6 churdles

METRIC/IMPERIAL

225 g/8 oz short crust pastry
(see page 69)

for filling

1 onion, chopped

175 g/6 oz lamb's liver

25 g/1 oz dripping

175 g/6 oz bacon pieces

50 g/2 oz mushrooms, chopped

1 small cooking apple, chopped

1 tablespoon chopped parsley

salt and pepper

1 tablespoon browned crumbs

1 tablespoon grated cheese

for garnish

tomato halves

parsley sprigs

Lightly fry onion and liver in the dripping for a few minutes, then mince or chop finely with the bacon pieces. Add mushrooms, apple and parsley. Season with salt and pepper.

Roll out pastry on lightly floured board.

With an up-turned saucer as guide, cut six pastry circles. Brush outside edges with water or milk. Divide filling mixture into six and place one portion on each circle. Pinch up edges to make three-cornered hat shape, leaving filling exposed in centre; stand churdles on a baking tray. Brush pastry with water or milk. Mix crumbs and cheese and sprinkle over churdles. Bake in a moderately hot oven for 40 minutes or until golden brown. Garnish with tomato halves and parsley.

SHROPSHIRE FITCHETT PIE

Cooking time   1 hour
Oven temperature   Hot
220°C, 425°F, Gas Mark 7 for 10 minutes;
moderately hot 190°C, 375°F, Gas Mark 5 for 40 minutes
Serves 4

METRIC/IMPERIAL

225 g/8 oz flaky pastry (see
  page 69)
for filling
25 g/1 oz cooking fat
225 g/8 oz bacon, coarsely
  chopped

225 g/8 oz onions, peeled and
  sliced into rings
450 g/1 lb cooking apples,
  peeled, cored and sliced
1 tablespoon black treacle
1 tablespoon hot water
salt and pepper

Melt fat in a pan, add bacon and onions and fry gently for about 10 minutes until soft but not crisp. Fill a medium-size pie dish with alternate layers of apples and fried bacon and onions, then add treacle mixed with water. Sprinkle lightly with salt and pepper. Damp edges of pie dish with water. Roll out pastry on lightly floured board and cover the pie; trim, rough up and flute edges. Brush with beaten egg and bake in centre of a hot oven for 10 minutes, then turn down oven to moderately hot and bake for another 40 minutes.

WELSH RAREBIT

Cooking time   about 8 minutes Serves 4

METRIC/IMPERIAL

25 g/1 oz butter
1 level tablespoon flour
3 tablespoons milk
2 tablespoons beer
1 teaspoon mixed mustard
few drops Worcestershire sauce

100–175 g/4–6 oz Cheddar
  cheese, grated
salt and pepper
4 slices hot buttered toast
for garnish
few tomato slices

Melt fat in pan and stir in flour, add milk and continue stirring until mixture forms a thick smooth sauce. Then add the beer, mustard, Worcestershire sauce, cheese and season to taste. Do not overcook. Spread mixture on buttered toast and put under a hot grill until golden brown. Top each with a tomato slice.

KENT APPLE SCONE

Cooking time   30 minutes
Oven temperature   Moderately hot
200°C, 400°F, Gas Mark 6
Makes 8 wedges

METRIC/IMPERIAL

2 medium cooking apples	110 g/4 oz butter
450 g/1 lb self-raising flour	110 g/4 oz castor sugar
1 teaspoon salt	300 ml/½ pint milk
2 teaspoons baking powder	1 tablespoon sieved apricot jam

Peel, core and finely chop one apple. Sift together the flour, salt and baking powder. Rub in butter, then add castor sugar and chopped apple. Mix to a soft, but not sticky, dough with milk. Roll out to a 20-cm/8-inch circle and place on a floured baking tray.

Mark top into eight wedges. Peel and core remaining apple and cut into thin slices. Brush top of scone with milk and arrange apple slices on top.

Bake in a moderately hot oven for about 30 minutes. While still hot, brush apple slices with apricot jam. Serve warm with butter.

NORFOLK SCONE

Cooking time   about 50 minutes
Oven temperature   Moderately hot
200°C, 400°F, Gas mark 6
Makes 8 wedges

METRIC/IMPERIAL

450 g/ 1 lb self-raising flour	*for filling*
1 teaspoon salt	25 g/1 oz softened butter or
110 g/4 oz butter or margarine	margarine
2 eggs	110 g/4 oz currants
250 ml/8 fl oz milk	½ teaspoon grated nutmeg
	110 g/4 oz demerara sugar

Sift together the flour and salt. Rub in butter or margarine until mixture resembles fine breadcrumbs. Mix to a soft dough with the eggs and milk beaten together. Turn on to a floured board and knead lightly. Divide in half and roll each out into a 20-cm/8-inch circle. Lift one circle on to a baking sheet and spread top with the softened butter.

Mix currants, nutmeg and 75 g/3 oz sugar together and sprinkle this mixture over butter. Place second circle on top, mark and cut through into eight wedges. Brush with milk and sprinkle over with remaining sugar. Bake in a moderately hot oven for about 50 minutes.

SOMERSET APPLES

Cooking time   35–40 minutes
Oven temperature   Moderately hot
190°C, 375°F, Gas Mark 5
Serves 4

METRIC/IMPERIAL

4 cooking apples	a few glacé cherries
25 g/1 oz butter	25 g/1 oz butter
for stuffing	*for glaze*
100 g/4 oz seedless raisins	2 tablespoons redcurrant jelly
50 g/2 oz almonds, blanched	2 tablespoons rose hip syrup
50 g/2 oz demerara sugar	

Wipe the apples and remove cores, stand them in an ovenproof dish. Mix together raisins, almonds and sugar and stuff apples with this mixture. Arrange cherries on top of apples and place a knob of butter on each. Bake in a moderately hot oven for 35–40 minutes.

Heat the redcurrant jelly and rose hip syrup together and pour over cooked apples.

SUSSEX POND PUDDING

Cooking time   2½–3 hours
Serves 4

METRIC/IMPERIAL

for suet crust pastry	50 g/2 oz currants
225 g/8 oz self-raising flour	150 ml/¼ pint water
1 teaspoon salt	*for filling*
75 g/3 oz shredded suet	225 g/8 oz butter
50 g/2 oz castor sugar	100 g/4 oz demerara sugar

Sift together the flour and salt. Mix in the suet, sugar and currants, add the water. Mix to a soft dough with a round-bladed knife. Lightly knead on a floured board until pastry is smooth. Divide pastry in half and roll each piece to a 15-cm/6-inch circle. Blend together butter and demerara sugar and mould into a ball. Put ball in centre of one round. Gather up edges of crust and enclose butter ball, then cover with second circle and pinch edges together. Grease a piece of 45-cm/18-inch square kitchen foil, tie up pudding tightly and steam for 2½–3 hours.

SOMERSET BRAMBLE AND APPLE PIE

Cooking time   40 minutes
Oven temperature   Moderately hot
190°C, 375°F, Gas Mark 5
Serves 4

METRIC/IMPERIAL

225 g/8 oz short crust pastry
  (see page 69)
beaten egg or milk
for filling
450 g/1 lb dessert apples

25 g/1 oz sugar
juice of 1 lemon
175 g/6 oz bramble jelly
25 g/1 oz chopped nuts

Line a shallow pie dish with rolled-out pastry, trim and flute edges
and bake blind (see page 68) in centre of a moderately hot oven for
25 minutes. Cut fruit-leaf shapes from pastry trimmings, glaze with
beaten egg or milk and bake at the same time as pastry case.

Core and slice apples but do not skin. Place apples, sugar and
lemon juice in a pan and cook over low heat for 10 minutes. Add
bramble jelly and cook for a further 4 minutes. Allow to cool. Turn
apple filling into baked pastry case. Sprinkle with chopped nuts and
decorate with pastry fruit leaves.

DEVONSHIRE SPLITS

Cooking time   10–15 minutes
Oven temperature   Moderately hot
200°C, 400°F, Gas Mark 6
Makes 24 splits

METRIC/IMPERIAL

350 g/12 oz self-raising flour
pinch salt
125 g/4½ oz margarine
75 g/3 oz castor sugar
about 4 tablespoons milk

to serve
about 50–75 g/2–3 oz butter
3 tablespoons strawberry jam
100 g/4 oz Devonshire clotted
  cream or 150 ml/¼ pint double
  cream, whipped

Sift the flour and salt into a bowl, rub in the margarine with the
fingertips until mixture resembles fine breadcrumbs. Stir in castor

sugar, mix to a stiff dough with the milk. Knead until smooth and free from cracks.

Roll out dough on a lightly floured board to 2 cm/¾ inch thick. Cut into 6-cm/2½-inch rounds. Place on a greased baking tray and bake on shelf above the centre of a moderately hot oven for about 10–15 minutes, until well risen and cooked through. Transfer to a wire rack, allow to cool. Split or cut in half, spread with butter, serve with strawberry jam and clotted or whipped double cream.

YORKSHIRE PARKIN

Cooking time   1½ hours
Oven temperature   Cool
140°C, 275°F, Gas Mark 1
Makes 1 parkin

METRIC/IMPERIAL

110 g/4 oz plain flour	350 g/12 oz oatmeal
good pinch salt	110 g/4 oz margarine
1 teaspoon ground ginger	275 g/10 oz golden syrup
½ teaspoon nutmeg	½ teaspoon bicarbonate of soda
110 g/4 oz soft brown sugar	2 tablespoons milk

Line the base of an oblong baking tin with kitchen foil. Sift the flour, salt, ginger and nutmeg together into a bowl. Add brown sugar and oatmeal. Heat margarine and syrup gently until the margarine has melted, then stir into dry ingredients and beat well. Dissolve bicarbonate of soda in milk, beat into mixture.

Turn into prepared tin and bake in a cool oven for 1½ hours, or until cooked through. When cold turn on to a wire rack.

Note Cut into squares. Keep for few days in airtight tin before eating.

NORTH COUNTRY MINT PASTIES

Cooking time   20 minutes
Oven temperature   Moderately hot
200°C, 400°F, Gas Mark 6
Serves 4

METRIC/IMPERIAL

225 g/8 oz short crust pastry
  (see page 69)
for filling
50 g/2 oz mixed peel
50 g/2 oz currants
50 g/2 oz demerara sugar

25 g/1 oz butter, melted
2 tablespoons fresh mint, finely
  chopped
for glaze
milk

Divide the pastry into four and roll each piece to a 15-cm/6-inch circle. Mix filling ingredients together and divide equally among rounds. Wet pastry edges really well and fold over. Press edges firmly together and crimp with the finger and thumb. Brush with milk and bake in a moderately hot oven for about 20 minutes, until golden brown. Serve hot or cold.

FEN COUNTRY SWEET POTATO CAKE

Cooking time   about 30 minutes
Oven temperature   Moderately hot
190°C, 375°F, Gas Mark 5
Serves 4

METRIC/IMPERIAL

450 g/1 lb cooked potatoes
100 g/4 oz castor sugar
100 g/4 oz candied peel, finely
  chopped

50 g/2 oz butter, melted
few drops vanilla essence
2 eggs
castor sugar to sprinkle on top

Grease a sandwich tin. Sieve the cooked potatoes into a basin, stir in sugar, peel, butter and essence. Separate the eggs and add beaten yolks to mixture. Fold in the stiffly whisked egg whites. If the mixture appears to be dry, a little milk may be added. Turn mixture into prepared pan, smooth top and bake in a moderately hot oven until nicely browned.

Turn out, sprinkle with sugar and serve very hot.

SCOTCH PANCAKES

Cooking time   about 7 minutes
Makes 16 pancakes

METRIC/IMPERIAL

110 g/4 oz plain flour	2 tablespoons castor sugar
1 teaspoon cream tartar	1 egg
½ teaspoon bicarbonate of soda	about 150 ml/¼ pint milk
good pinch salt	

Sift the flour, cream of tartar, bicarbonate of soda and salt together into a mixing bowl. Stir in sugar. Make a well in the centre and drop in the egg with a little of the milk. Mix well, gradually drawing in the flour from the sides of the bowl. Gradually add the remaining milk to make a smooth batter.

Lightly grease a griddle, heavy frying pan or solid electric hot-plate, and place on spoonfuls of the prepared batter. Pour from the tip of the spoon to give a good round shape. Cook until the surface of the scones is full of bubbles and the underside is golden brown. Turn over with a palette knife and cook on the other side. Serve at once with butter, or place between folds of a teatowel until required.

HIGHLAND SHORTBREAD

Cooking time   1 hour
Oven temperature   Cool
150°C, 300°F, Gas Mark 2
Makes 2 rounds

METRIC/IMPERIAL

350 g/12 oz plain flour	225 g/8 oz butter
110 g/4 oz castor sugar	castor sugar to dredge
good pinch salt	

Place the flour, sugar and salt on a large board or table surface. (If this is not possible, a bowl may be used.) Make a well in the centre and put in the butter which has been cut into large pieces. Gradually work the dry ingredients into the butter with tips of the fingers to form a smooth paste. Knead lightly, divide into two, roll into rounds 2 cm/¾ inch thick and transfer to lightly greased baking trays.

Prick surfaces with a fork and pinch up edges. Mark lightly into triangles with a knife and bake on centre shelf of a cool oven for

1 hour, or until pale golden in colour and cooked through. Transfer to a wire rack and allow to cool. Sprinkle with castor sugar and when cold break into triangles, if liked.

Note Store in an airtight tin until required.

DUNDEE CAKE

Cooking time   2½–3 hours
Oven temperature   Moderate
180°C, 350°F, Gas Mark 4 for 1 hour;
cool 140°C, 275°F, Gas Mark 1 for 1½–2 hours

METRIC/IMPERIAL

275 g/10 oz plain flour	25 g/1 oz chopped almonds
¼ teaspoon bicarbonate of soda	225 g/8 oz sultanas
good pinch salt	225 g/8 oz currants
225 g/8 oz butter	50 g/2 oz chopped glacé cherries
225 g/8 oz castor sugar	50 g/2 oz chopped mixed peel
4 eggs	50–75 g/2–2½ oz split blanched
grated rind of 1 orange	almonds

Line a greased 20-cm/8-inch round tin with greased greaseproof paper. Sift the flour, bicarbonate of soda and salt together. Cream butter and sugar together until light and fluffy. Lightly whisk the eggs, then beat well into creamed mixture, a little at a time, with a little of the sifted flour, if necessary, to prevent curdling. Stir in grated orange rind and fold in remaining flour. Carefully stir in chopped almonds, sultanas, currants, cherries and mixed peel until thoroughly mixed.

Turn into the prepared tin and smooth top of the mixture with a palette knife. Make a shallow dip in the centre of the cake and lay the split almonds on top in a neat design.

Cook towards centre of a moderate oven for approximately 1 hour, then reduce oven temperature to cool for about 1½–2 hours, or until cake is well risen and cooked through – test with a skewer. It may be necessary to cover the top of the cake after 2 hours to prevent it from over-browning.

Note This cake will keep well in an airtight tin for up to two weeks before cutting.

IRISH SODA BREAD

Cooking time   35–45 minutes
Oven temperature Hot
220°C, 425°F, Gas Mark 7
Makes 1 675-g/1½-lb loaf

METRIC/IMPERIAL

450 g/1 lb plain flour
1 teaspoon salt
2 teaspoons bicarbonate of soda

300–400 ml/½–¾ pint soured milk
or buttermilk

Sift the flour, salt and bicarbonate of soda into a bowl. Make a well in the centre and pour in a generous 300 ml/½ pint soured milk or buttermilk. Mix with a knife to a soft dough. If the dough seems a little dry, cut in a little more liquid through the centre of the dough using a knife.

Knead lightly with the fingertips to a round shape. Turn smooth-side up, place on a floured baking tray and cut a deep cross on top to allow the bread to rise evenly.

Bake on shelf above centre in a hot oven for 35–45 minutes until well risen and lightly brown. When cooked, the loaf should sound hollow if tapped on base. Cool on a wire tray.

BARA BRITH (WELSH BUN LOAF)

Cooking time   1–1¼ hours
Oven temperature   Moderately hot
190°C, 375°F, Gas Mark 5
Makes 1 loaf

METRIC/IMPERIAL

450 g/1 lb plain flour
½ teaspoon salt
75 g/3 oz butter or margarine
110 g/4 oz sugar

175 g/6 oz mixed dried fruit
15 g/½ oz dried yeast
150 ml/¼ pint warm water
150 ml/¼ pint warm milk

Sift the flour and salt into a bowl. Rub in the fat lightly. Mix in all but 1 teaspoon of sugar and cleaned dried fruit. Place yeast, rest of sugar and warm water in a jug and stand in a warm place until frothy on top, about 10 minutes. Add to flour mixture together with warm milk to make a soft dough. Knead for a few minutes, then cover bowl and leave in a warm place until dough is doubled in size and springs back when pressed with floured finger, about 1½ hours. Turn on to a lightly floured board and knead for about 10 minutes.

Shape dough and place in lightly greased 1-kg/2-lb loaf tin. Cover tin and leave in a warm place to rise for about 30 minutes. Bake just below centre in a moderately hot oven for 1–1¼ hours until well browned and loaf sounds hollow when tapped. Serve thinly sliced, spread with butter.

LINCOLNSHIRE PLUM BREAD

Cooking time   3 hours
Oven temperature   Very cool
120°C, 250°F, Gas Mark ½
Makes 1 loaf

METRIC/IMPERIAL

110 g/4 oz butter	200 g/7 oz self-raising flour
110 g/4 oz demerara sugar	pinch salt
¾ teaspoon powdered cinnamon	110 g/4 oz prunes, steeped for 2
½ teaspoon mixed spice	days in cold water and finely
½ teaspoon liquid gravy	chopped
browning	110 g/4 oz currants
2 eggs	110 g/4 oz sultanas
1 tablespoon brandy	

Grease and line a 1-kg/2-lb loaf tin. Cream the fat and sugar together until light and fluffy, beat in spices, browning, eggs and brandy gradually. Sift in flour and salt. Stir in prepared fruit. Turn into prepared tin and bake in very cool oven for about 3 hours, or until cooked through.

Turn out and cool on a wire rack.

Egg, Cheese and Salad Dishes

One of the most traditional meals in all the land is the ploughman's lunch: a hearty chunk of good farmhouse cheese with crusty bread. And if you have a bowl of new-laid eggs and fresh salad available you lack nothing for a feast. An appetite keened by fresh air can be easily satisfied by this simple but delicious fare.

Egg Dishes

FARMER'S OMELETTE

Cooking time   about 20 minutes
Serves 1

METRIC/IMPERIAL

1 large raw potato	2 eggs
25 g/1 oz butter	salt and pepper
50 g/2 oz Cheddar cheese	few chopped chives

Peel the potato and cut into very small dice. Melt the butter in an omelette pan and cook potato, shaking often until golden brown and crisp all over. Add cheese cut into small dice. Pour the lightly beaten, well-seasoned eggs over the potato and cheese and cook until almost set. Place under a hot grill for 2–3 minutes to set the top, then transfer to a serving dish and sprinkle with a few chopped chives.

Variations

Add 1 small onion, finely chopped, to potato.
Add sprinkling of dried mixed herbs to potato and cheese mixture.

FRIED BACON AND EGG FINGERS

Cooking time   about 10 minutes
Serves 4

METRIC/IMPERIAL

8 bacon rashers	salt and pepper
2 eggs	2 thick slices white bread

Fry the bacon, adding a little extra fat to the pan if necessary. Beat the eggs well and season. Cut the bread into fingers and dip in egg until soaked through. Fry in hot bacon fat until crisp and golden on both sides. Serve with the bacon.

EGGS VICTORIANA

Cooking time   about 30 minutes
Oven temperature   Hot
220°C, 425°F, Gas Mark 7
Serves 4

METRIC/IMPERIAL

4 hard-boiled eggs, sliced	400 ml/scant ¾ pint milk
25 g/1 oz butter	salt and pepper
1 large onion, finely sliced	100–175 g/4–6 oz Cheddar
25 g/1 oz plain flour	cheese, grated

Arrange the hard-boiled eggs in base of a shallow ovenproof dish. Keep warm. Melt the butter in a saucepan, add onion, and fry gently until completely tender, but not browned. Stir in the flour and cook for a minute. Remove from heat and stir in milk gradually. Return to heat and bring to the boil, stirring. Cook for a minute, season, and pour over eggs in the dish. Sprinkle cheese over top, and place in a hot oven for about 20 minutes to brown.

SHIRRED EGGS

Cooking time   about 10 minutes
Oven temperature   Moderate
180°C, 350°F, Gas Mark 4
Serves 4

METRIC/IMPERIAL

50 g/2 oz butter	*for garnish*
4 eggs	parsley sprigs
salt and pepper	

Divide the butter equally between four small fireproof dishes. Heat until butter bubbles. Break each egg into a cup, then transfer to a dish. Sprinkle with salt and pepper and bake in a moderate oven for 10 minutes, or until whites of eggs are set. Garnish with a sprig of parsley on each.

BAKED EGG CUSTARD

Cooking time 30–40 minutes
Oven temperature Cool
150°C, 300°F, Gas Mark 2
Serves 4

METRIC/IMPERIAL

2 eggs   600 ml/1 pint milk
25 g/1 oz castor sugar   little grated nutmeg

Beat the eggs and sugar lightly. Add the milk and mix well until the sugar is dissolved. Strain into a greased pie dish. Grate a little nutmeg over the top. Bake in the middle of a cool oven for 30–40 minutes.

EGG AND FISH SCRAMBLE

Cooking time about 3 minutes
Serves 4

METRIC/IMPERIAL

100 g/4 oz boned cooked fish   salt and pepper
  (any white fish, smoked   25 g/1 oz butter
  haddock or kipper)   4 rounds buttered toast
3 eggs   *for garnish*
1 tablespoon milk   little chopped parsley
pinch dry mustard

Flake the fish finely. Whisk the eggs, milk and seasonings together then stir in prepared fish. Melt the butter in a saucepan. Pour in mixture and stir continually until lightly scrambled. Pile on to rounds of buttered toast and sprinkle top with a little parsley.

SCOTCH EGGS

Cooking time   about 5 minutes
Serves 4

METRIC/IMPERIAL

4 hard-boiled eggs	225 g/8 oz sausage meat
1 tablespoon seasoned flour	1 egg
few drops Worcestershire or	fresh breadcrumbs
other piquant sauce	fat for deep frying

Shell the eggs, dip in seasoned flour. Add a few drops of Worcestershire or other sauce to the sausage meat and mix well together.

Divide into four and cover each egg completely with the mixture. Coat in beaten egg and breadcrumbs. Fry in deep hot fat until golden brown all over, giving enough cooking time to cook the sausage meat right through (about 5 minutes). Drain well on kitchen paper. Cut in half lengthwise, and serve hot with tomato sauce and vegetables or cold with salad.

HOPEL POPEL

Cooking time   about 10 minutes
Serves 4

METRIC/IMPERIAL

50 g/2 oz butter	450 g/1 lb boiled potatoes, diced
100 g/4 oz streaky bacon, diced	4 eggs
1 onion, finely chopped	salt and pepper
100 g/4 oz mushrooms, chopped	50 g/2 oz Cheddar cheese, grated

Melt the butter in a frying pan, add the bacon, onion and mushrooms, fry gently for a few minutes until tender. Add the potatoes and allow to warm through. Beat the eggs with seasoning and pour them over mixture, sprinkle with grated cheese and cook slowly until the eggs are set. Brown the top under the grill for a minute or two. Serve hot cut in wedges.

QUICK SALAD DRESSING

4 tablespoons olive oil

2 tablespoons wine vinegar

¼ teaspoon each: dry
 mustard, salt, sugar, pepper

2–3 hard-boiled eggs

1 tablespoon chopped parsley

Place oil, vinegar, mustard, salt, sugar and pepper in a screw-topped jar and shake until thoroughly blended. Shell and finely chop the eggs, then stir into the dressing together with the parsley just before serving. Serve with cold meat or fish salads.

EGG SAUCE

15 g/½ oz butter or margarine

15 g/½ oz plain flour

300 ml/½ pint milk

small pinch cayenne pepper

salt

2–3 hard-boiled eggs

Melt the fat in a small pan and stir in the flour. Gradually blend in the milk to make a smooth sauce. Add a pinch of cayenne and salt to taste. Bring to the boil, still stirring, and cook for 3 minutes. Shell and chop the eggs. Mix into the sauce and heat for a few seconds. Can be served with ham, bacon or fish dishes.

MAYONNAISE

Makes 150 ml/¼ pint mayonnaise

1 egg yolk

¼ teaspoon each: salt, pepper,
 dry mustard

1 teaspoon castor sugar

1 tablespoon tarragon vinegar or
 lemon juice

150 ml/¼ pint olive or corn oil

Mix the egg yolk, seasonings and sugar together in a bowl. Stir in 1 teaspoon vinegar or lemon juice, and whisk. Add half the oil drop by drop, whisking well after each addition. Add remaining oil in a thin stream, whisking all the time until the mixture is thick and creamy. Gradually stir in the remaining vinegar or lemon juice.

Note 2 tablespoons whipped cream may be added, if liked.

Cheese Dishes

CREAMY CHEESE AND ONION SOUP

Cooking time   about 15 minutes
Serves 4

METRIC/IMPERIAL

25 g/1 oz butter	salt and pepper
450 g/1 lb onions, thinly sliced	175 g/6 oz Cheddar cheese,
25 g/1 oz plain flour	grated
600 ml/1 pint milk	*for garnish*
450 ml/¾ pint water	chopped parsley

Melt the butter in a large saucepan. Add onions and gently fry until tender but not browned, about 10 minutes. Add the flour and cook for a minute, stirring. Gradually stir in milk and water and bring to the boil. Season, and cook for 2 minutes. Remove from the heat, stir in cheese until it has melted. Garnish with chopped parsley to serve.

CHEESE AND SHRIMP SOUP

Cooking time   about 10–15 minutes
Serves 4

METRIC/IMPERIAL

1 large onion, finely chopped	1 teaspoon lemon juice
50 g/2 oz butter	1 teaspoon Worcestershire sauce
25 g/1 oz flour	225 g/8 oz Cheddar cheese,
600 ml/1 pint milk	finely grated
600 ml/1 pint stock	50 g/2 oz peeled shrimps
salt and pepper	100 g/4 oz cooked green peas
dry mustard	

Lightly sauté onion in melted butter until tender. Add the flour and, stirring, cook gently for about a minute. Add the milk gradually, stir constantly until the sauce has thickened. Whisk in the stock, and season. Bring to the boil, stir in cheese, shrimps and peas. Remove from heat and continue stirring until cheese has dissolved. Serve at once.

TOMATO CHEESE TOASTIES

Cooking time   7 minutes
Serves 4

METRIC/IMPERIAL

20 g/¾ oz butter
20 g/¾ oz flour
300 ml/½ pint milk
½ teaspoon prepared mustard
cayenne pepper

225 g/8 oz Cheddar cheese,
  grated
4 slices buttered toast
4 tomatoes, skinned and sliced
2 rashers bacon, cut across in half

Melt the butter, add the flour and cook for a minute. Remove from heat. Add the milk gradually, stirring, bring to the boil and cook for a minute. Remove from heat, add the seasonings and grated cheese and stir until the cheese has melted. Prepare the toast and grill the bacon. Arrange the tomato slices on the toast and put under the grill to heat through. Pour the hot cheese sauce over and garnish with crisp pieces of bacon.

POTATO CHEESE PIE

Cooking time   1 hour
Oven temperature   Moderate
180°C, 350°F, Gas Mark 4
Serves 4

METRIC/IMPERIAL

225 g/8 oz Cheddar cheese,
  grated
1 kg/2 lb raw potatoes, thinly
  sliced
25 g/1 oz butter

300 ml/½ pint milk
salt and pepper
2 eggs
breadcrumbs
¼ teaspoon grated nutmeg

Put alternate layers of grated cheese and thinly sliced potatoes into a buttered fireproof dish, ending with grated cheese. Melt the butter in the milk, season well and pour on to the well beaten eggs. Pour this mixture over the potato and cheese, add a sprinkling of breadcrumbs and a little nutmeg, if liked. Bake in a moderate oven for about 1 hour, until the potatoes are cooked and the top nicely brown. Serve hot.

CHEESE BAKED POTATOES

Cooking time 1¼–1½ hours
Oven temperature Moderate
180°C, 350°F, Gas Mark 4
Serves 4

METRIC/IMPERIAL

4 medium potatoes	100 g/4 oz Cheddar cheese,
2 tablespoons milk	grated
good pinch salt and cayenne	1 tablespoon chopped parsley
pepper	

Wash and scrub the potatoes, and prick with a fork. Bake in a moderate oven until they feel soft when pinched, about 1¼–1½ hours. Cut each potato in half and scoop out the cooked part, mash with a fork. Beat in the milk, seasonings and lastly the grated cheese and chopped parsley. Return the mixture to the potato-skin shells and reheat in the oven for a few minutes. Serve on their own, or with cold meat.

PAN HAGGERTY

Cooking time 30 minutes
Serves 4

METRIC/IMPERIAL

450 g/1 lb peeled potatoes	175 g/6 oz Cheddar cheese,
225 g/8 oz onions	grated
25 g/1 oz butter	salt and pepper

Slice the potatoes very thinly and dry off in a cloth. Slice onions thinly. Melt the butter in a frying pan and put in a layer of potato, the onions, then grated cheese, and finish with another layer of potato. Season between each layer. Fry gently for about 25 minutes, or until cooked, then place under grill for a further 5 minutes to brown.

ASPARAGUS WITH CHEESE SAUCE

Cooking time   about 7 minutes
Serves 4

METRIC/IMPERIAL

450 g/1 lb cooked green
  asparagus tips
for sauce
2 tablespoons water
2 teaspoons wine vinegar
2 egg yolks

50 g/2 oz butter
salt and cayenne pepper
2 teaspoons lemon juice
75 g/3 oz Cheddar cheese, grated
for garnish
paprika pepper

Arrange the drained asparagus on a serving dish. Cover and keep
warm. Put water, wine vinegar and egg yolks in a bowl over a pan
of hot water and whisk well until thickened. Whisk in the butter in
small pieces, then add seasonings, lemon juice and cheese, and mix
thoroughly. Spoon sauce over asparagus, and garnish with paprika
pepper.

CHEESE MEDLEY

Cooking time   1 hour 10 minutes
Oven temperature   Moderately hot
190°C, 375°F, Gas Mark 5
Serves 4

METRIC/IMPERIAL

40 g/1½ oz butter
3 medium onions, sliced
1 medium swede, sliced
450 g/ 1 lb carrots, sliced
salt and pepper
225 g/8 oz back bacon rashers,
  cut into quarters
for sauce
25 g/1 oz butter
25 g/1 oz plain flour

300 ml/½ pint milk
100 g/4 oz Cheddar cheese,
  grated
salt and pepper
pinch of ground nutmeg
for topping
50 g/2 oz Cheddar cheese,
  grated
25 g/1 oz browned crumbs

Melt the butter in a large frying pan, and gently fry onions, swede
and carrots for about 20 minutes, turning frequently. Season. Turn
half the vegetable mixture into a large ovenproof dish and cover with

pieces of bacon. Arrange remaining vegetable mixture over bacon.

For sauce

Melt butter in a small pan, add flour and cook for a minute. Remove from heat, and stir in milk gradually. Return to heat and bring to the boil, stirring. Cook for a minute, remove from heat, and stir in the cheese, seasonings and nutmeg. Stir until cheese has melted, and pour sauce over vegetables in dish. Top with cheese and crumbs mixed together, and bake in a moderately hot oven about 45 minutes, until top is browned and vegetables completely tender.

CAULIFLOWER CHEESE

Cooking time   about 30 minutes
Serves 4

METRIC/IMPERIAL

1 cauliflower	½ teaspoon salt
for cheese sauce	1 teaspoon made mustard
25 g/1 oz butter	pinch nutmeg
25 g/1 oz plain flour	*for topping*
300 ml/½ pint milk (or milk and cauliflower water)	25 g/1 oz grated Cheddar cheese
75 g/3 oz Cheddar cheese, grated	1 tablespoon browned crumbs

Soak the cauliflower in cold water for about 15 minutes, then break into flowerets. Cook in a little boiling water in a covered pan until tender, and arrange neatly in buttered scallop shells or a fireproof dish.

For cheese sauce

Melt the butter, add the flour and cook for 1 minute. Remove from heat and add the milk gradually. Bring to the boil, stirring well. Cook for a minute, remove from the heat, add the seasonings and grated Cheddar cheese, and stir until the cheese has melted. Coat the cauliflower with the cheese sauce. Sprinkle over it the mixed grated cheese and browned crumbs. Brown under a hot grill.

FARMHOUSE CHEESE CAKE

Cooking time   about 35 minutes
Oven temperature   Moderately hot
190°C, 375°F, Gas Mark 5
Serves 4–6

METRIC/IMPERIAL

175 g/6 oz short crust pastry
(see page 69)
for filling
50 g/2 oz butter
25 g/1 oz castor sugar
1 beaten egg

175 g/6 oz Cheddar cheese,
finely grated
3 tablespoons milk
40 g/1½ oz seedless raisins
15 g/½ oz chopped mixed peel
grated rind of ½ lemon

Roll the pastry out thinly on a lightly floured board. Use to line a deep
pie plate, trim and decorate edges.

For filling

Cream the butter and sugar until light and fluffy, then add egg,
cheese, milk, raisins, peel and lemon rind. Mix well and turn into pie
plate. Decorate top of cheese cake with pastry trimmings. Bake in a
moderately hot oven for about 35 minutes. Cool and serve.

PEARS TANSY

Serves 4–6

METRIC/IMPERIAL

150 ml/¼ pint soured cream
225 g/8 oz Cheddar cheese,
grated
4 tablespoons
blackcurrant jam

15 g/½ oz walnuts, chopped
3 large ripe pears
lemon juice
for decoration
walnut halves

Put the soured cream, cheese, blackcurrant jam and chopped walnuts
into a basin and mix well. Peel, halve and core pears, brush with
lemon juice, and arrange on a serving dish. Spoon filling on to
centres of pears, top each with a halved walnut, and serve as dessert.

Salad Dishes

NEW POTATO SALAD

Cooking time   15–20 minutes
Serves 4

METRIC/IMPERIAL

450 g/1 lb new potatoes
150 ml/¼ pint double cream
1 tablespoon lemon juice

salt and paprika pepper
1 tablespoon chopped chives

Scrub or scrape the potatoes and cook in boiling salted water until just tender, 15–20 minutes. Drain well and dice. Whip the cream, add lemon juice, potatoes, seasoning and chopped chives. Leave in refrigerator or cool place until ready to serve.

HOT POTATO SALAD

Cooking time   about 25 minutes
Serves 4

METRIC/IMPERIAL

450 g/1 lb potatoes
1 small onion, finely chopped
3 tablespoons salad oil

1 tablespoon malt vinegar
salt and pepper

Boil the potatoes gently in their skins until just cooked. Remove skins and cut potatoes into slices. Fry onion gently in oil for a few minutes until just soft, add vinegar and seasoning, pour it over the potatoes.

HAM SALAD

Serves 4

METRIC/IMPERIAL

450 g/1 lb potatoes, cooked
    and diced
225 g/8 oz beetroot, cooked and
    diced
3–4 tablespoons salad cream
1 lettuce

2 dessert apples
juice of ½ lemon
225 g/8 oz cooked ham
50 g/2 oz walnuts, chopped
2 teaspoons chopped parsley

Mix the potato and beetroot with enough salad cream to moisten. Wash and shred the lettuce. Peel, core and slice apples thinly, then sprinkle with lemon juice to preserve colour. Cut ham into thin strips. Combine apples, walnuts and ham, and place in two bands on a flat dish. Fill the middle with lettuce, and arrange bands of potato and beetroot salad sprinkled with chopped parsley on the outside.

COUNTRY SALAD

Serves 4

METRIC/IMPERIAL

1 bunch radishes	100 g/4 oz Leicester cheese
1 bunch spring onions	100 g/4 oz Wensleydale cheese
1 head endive	2 hard-boiled eggs
1 bunch watercress	paprika pepper

Wash all salad foods and drain well. Cut the radishes and spring onions into slices. Place endive and watercress in salad bowl and toss with radishes and onions. Cut cheese into small neat cubes; pile into centre of dish. Garnish with sliced hard-boiled eggs sprinkled with a little paprika pepper.

JANUARY SALAD

Cooking time 5 minutes
Serves 4

METRIC/IMPERIAL

225 g/8 oz beetroot, cooked	a little lemon juice
225 g/8 oz Bramley's Seedling apples	salt and pepper
	watercress
100 g/4 oz Cheddar cheese	8 rashers streaky bacon

Coarsely grate the peeled beetroot, apples and cheese. Mix together with lemon juice and seasoning. Serve on a bed of watercress on a flat dish. Cut off the bacon rinds, roll each rasher into a curl, grill quickly and lay on top of the salad.

SUMMER BEEF SALAD

Serves 4

METRIC/IMPERIAL

450 g/1 lb cold rare roast beef	lettuce
2 eating apples, peeled, cored and diced	endive
	for dressing
2 celery sticks, diced	6 tablespoons salad oil
4 shallots, finely chopped	2–3 tablespoons wine vinegar
1 small garlic clove, crushed	salt and freshly ground black
4 tablespoons finely chopped parsley	pepper

Trim and dice the beef. Combine beef, apples, celery, shallots with garlic and parsley. Line a salad bowl with leaves of lettuce and endive. Whisk oil with the vinegar and seasoning. Pour dressing over salad just before serving.

HARVEST SALAD

Serves 4

METRIC/IMPERIAL

300 ml/½ pint soured cream	450 g/1 lb fresh blackberries
few drops Tabasco sauce	1 tablespoon castor sugar
pinch dry mustard	225 g/8 oz Cheddar cheese,
salt and pepper	coarsely grated
2 tablespoons lemon juice	*for garnish*
3 medium eating apples	paprika pepper

Mix together soured cream, Tabasco sauce, mustard, seasonings, and half the lemon juice. Peel, core and slice apples, and sprinkle with remaining lemon juice. Mix blackberries with castor sugar.

Arrange half the apple in base of a deep serving dish, cover with half the blackberries, then half the cheese and half the soured cream mixture. Continue layers with remaining ingredients finishing with soured cream mixture on top. Garnish with paprika pepper. Serve with cooked cold ham or pork.

MUSHROOM CREAM SALAD

Serves 4

METRIC/IMPERIAL

100 g/4 oz mushrooms
3 hard-boiled eggs
¼ peeled cucumber
½ teaspoon dry mustard
½ teaspoon grated horseradish

150 ml/¼ pint thick soured cream
salt and pepper
lettuce
4 tomatoes, sliced

Finely chop the mushrooms, eggs and cucumber. Blend mustard and horseradish with the cream, adding salt and pepper. Stir in the chopped ingredients. Arrange lettuce leaves on a dish, spoon in cream mixture and circle with tomato slices.

TOMATO DELIGHTS

Serves 4

METRIC/IMPERIAL

8 large firm tomatoes
225 g/8 oz boiled potatoes
2 tablespoons salad cream
1 tablespoon chopped parsley

300 ml/½ pint prawns or shrimps
parsley to garnish
small lettuce

Wipe the tomatoes with a clean cloth. Stand stalk end down and cut off each top with a sharp knife. Use handle of a teaspoon to scoop out pulp into a dish. Mix drained pulp with finely diced potatoes, salad cream and chopped parsley.

Peel prawns or shrimps, reserving heads for decoration. Leave eight prawns or shrimps whole. Chop remainder finely; add to potato mixture. Pile into tomato cases and top each with whole prawn or shrimp and a small sprig of parsley. Arrange on a bed of lettuce and garnish with a few prawn heads.

Fish Ways

Traditionally, the people of Britain have a stirring history as seafarers and fishermen. As a nation, we have access to nourishing and delicious sea foods, and with modern methods of marketing and storing, a wide variety of good fish, either fresh or frozen, is obtainable in all parts of the country.

Fish is a very nutritious food with a high protein content. Here are some tips on care and cooking.

If possible eat fresh fish on the day of purchase. If it has to be stored overnight, wash and put it in a clean covered container in a refrigerator or cold larder. Frozen fish may be stored for two or three days in the cold compartment of the refrigerator, or according to the directions on the packet, but once thawed out it must not be refrozen and should be cooked within 24 hours.

To scale fish hold by the tail and scrape very firmly with the back of a knife towards the head.

To skin fillets take the fillet in the left hand, skin side down, holding it by the tip. Make a firm cut with a sharp knife at the tip, then lift away from the skin, continuing until all flesh is free. Dip the knife edge in salt for a better cutting edge.

Never over-cook fish as the flavour is easily lost. Fish is cooked when the flesh has just shrunk away from the bone or skin, or in the case of fillets the flakes should separate easily.

To poach fish means to simmer gently in salted water or fish stock. Suitable for large fish, like salmon and haddock, having a strong flavour.

Grilling is an excellent method for fillets, cutlets and small whole fish. The prepared fish should always be brushed with a little oil or melted fat, and may be sprinkled with coarse oatmeal or dried breadcrumbs. The grill should be pre-heated before the fish is placed under it.

Baking is a tasty method for most kinds of fish.

Steamed fish is often recommended for invalids because it is so easy to digest. Season and sprinkle with lemon juice before steaming, drain well and serve with a plain sauce or garnish.

OCEAN PIE

Cooking time   30 minutes
Oven temperature   Hot
220°C, 425°F, Gas Mark 7
Serves 4

METRIC/IMPERIAL

225 g/8 oz smoked haddock	75 g/3 oz prawns, peeled
2 scallops	300 ml/½ pint white sauce (see
100 g/4 oz soft roes	page 45)
salt and pepper	4 tablespoons thick cream
100 g/4 oz mushrooms	1 kg/2 lb fluffy, creamed potatoes

Cut the haddock into 7-cm/3-in squares. Clean and chop the scallops and roes, and arrange in a fireproof dish. Season. Place the haddock on top. Slice the mushrooms and add with the prawns to the white sauce. Simmer for 5 minutes, then stir in the cream away from the heat. Pour the sauce over the fish and top with creamy potatoes. Cook in a hot oven for about 25 minutes.

COUNTRY FISH PIE

Cooking time   about 30 minutes
Serves 4

METRIC/IMPERIAL

675 g/1½ lb cod fillet	2 tablespoons chopped parsley
about 600 ml/1 pint water to	2 hard-boiled eggs
cover	*for topping*
strip lemon rind	450 g/1 lb freshly boiled potatoes
1 bay leaf	25 g/1 oz cheese, finely grated
salt and pepper	*for garnish*
50 g/2 oz butter or margarine	1 tomato, sliced
40 g/1½ oz plain flour	parsley sprigs
300 ml/½ pint milk	

Wipe the cod and place in a large saucepan with water to cover. Add the lemon rind, bay leaf and salt and pepper. Bring to the boil, then simmer gently for about 15 minutes. Remove the fish with a draining spoon, discard any skin and bones and flake into small pieces.

Melt the butter or margarine in a saucepan. Sprinkle in the flour and cook for 2 minutes, stirring. Gradually blend in the milk and 150 ml/¼ pint strained fish liquor. Bring to the boil then simmer gently 2–3 minutes, stirring throughout to make a smooth sauce. Add the flaked fish, chopped parsley, and roughly chopped hard-boiled eggs. Season to taste if necessary. Pour into a deep pie dish or ovenproof dish. Cover with thinly sliced cooked potatoes and sprinkle with finely grated cheese. Place under a hot grill until golden brown and crisp. Decorate with chopped tomato and sprigs of parsley.

FINNAN HADDOCK IN MUSHROOM CREAM

Cooking time   30 minutes
Oven temperature   Moderately hot
190°C, 375°F, Gas Mark 5
Serves 4

METRIC/IMPERIAL

4 finnan haddock fillets	50 g/2 oz butter
225 g/8 oz mushrooms	150 ml/¼ pint double cream
freshly ground black pepper	*for garnish*
300 ml/½ pint milk	paprika, lemon wedges

Place the fillets in an ovenproof dish and slice the mushrooms over the top. Sprinkle generously with freshly ground black pepper, pour the milk over them and dot with butter. Cover the dish and bake in a moderately hot oven for about 25 minutes. Strain milk from the fish and mix with the cream: pour this mixture over the fish and replace in the oven for a few minutes to heat through. Serve with paprika and garnished with lemon wedges.

COD IN CIDER

Cooking time   30 minutes
Oven temperature   Moderately hot
190°C, 375°F, Gas Mark 5
Serves 4

METRIC/IMPERIAL

450 g/1 lb cod fillet	salt and pepper
100 g/4 oz mushrooms	25 g/1 oz butter
2 large tomatoes, halved	25 g/1 oz plain flour
300 ml/½ pint cider	50–75 g/2–3 oz cheese, grated

Cut the cod into four serving pieces, and arrange in a greased fireproof dish with the mushrooms and tomatoes. Pour the cider slowly over all the ingredients in the dish and then season them with salt and pepper. Bake for about 25 minutes in a moderately hot oven.

Meanwhile. melt the fat, add the flour and cook for a few minutes. Add the liquid from the fish, bring to the boil and cook gently, stirring, for a few minutes. Pour this sauce over the fish, sprinkle with the grated cheese and brown under a hot grill.

DEVILLED HALIBUT

Cooking time   25–35 minutes
Oven temperature   Moderately hot
190°C, 375°F, Gas Mark 5
Serves 4

METRIC/IMPERIAL

4 halibut steaks	½ teaspoon anchovy essence
75 g/3 oz butter or margarine	2 teaspoons made mustard
50–75 g/2–3 oz fresh breadcrumbs	1 tablespoon chopped piccalilli
150 ml/¼ pint thick white sauce (see below)	good pinch each: salt, pepper and cayenne

Wipe the halibut steaks and place in the base of the grill pan. Dot with 50 g/2 oz of the butter and cook under a medium grill for 10–15 minutes or until just tender. Transfer to an ovenproof dish, pour over them any juices from the pan. Place breadcrumbs on a baking sheet in a moderately hot oven for 5 minutes or until pale golden brown.

Blend thick white sauce, anchovy essence, made mustard, chopped piccalilli and seasonings together. Spread over fish steaks and sprinkle with browned breadcrumbs. Dot with remaining butter, bake in a moderately hot oven for 15–20 minutes. Serve very hot.

WHITE SAUCE

Makes 300 ml/½ pint sauce

METRIC/IMPERIAL

25 g/1 oz butter or margarine	300 ml/½ pint milk
25 g/1 oz plain flour	salt and pepper

Melt butter or margarine in a small pan, but do not allow it to brown. Remove from the heat, stir in the flour. Stir over gentle heat for about 1 minute until mixture bubbles and looks like a honeycomb. Remove the pan from heat and gradually blend in milk, a little at a time, beating well to avoid lumps. Season to taste. Return pan to gentle heat, bring to the boil and simmer gently, stirring all the time for 3 minutes, to form a smooth, glossy sauce, thick enough to coat the back of a spoon.

BUTTERED TROUT

Cooking time about 12 minutes
Serves 4

METRIC/IMPERIAL

4 medium trout	2 tablespoons lemon juice
1 tablespoon seasoned flour	1 tablespoon chopped parsley
100–175 g/4–6 oz butter	

Clean and gut the trout, wipe fish with a clean damp cloth, then toss them in seasoned flour to coat. Melt the butter in a frying pan and fry trout gently, turning once during the cooking, until nicely browned and cooked through, about 10 minutes. Transfer to a serving dish. Stir lemon juice and parsley into remaining butter in the pan and heat through; pour it over the fish.

GRILLED SALMON

Cooking time about 12–16 minutes
Serves 4

METRIC/IMPERIAL

4 salmon steaks (middle cut)	parsley butter (see below)
50 g/2 oz melted butter	*for garnish*
salt and pepper	lemon wedges

Wipe the fish with a clean damp cloth, then brush over with melted butter. Season to taste with salt and pepper and place the steaks on a well-greased grill rack. Grill each side 6–8 minutes, according to thickness of the slices or until steaks are cooked through.

Serve each steak topped with parsley butter. Garnish with lemon wedges.

PARSLEY BUTTER

METRIC/IMPERIAL

50 g/2 oz unsalted butter	few drops of lemon juice
2 teaspoons chopped parsley	salt and pepper

Soften the butter on a plate with a palette knife, then work in the parsley, lemon juice and seasoning to taste. Serve chilled in pats.

Note Also suitable for serving with mixed grills and steak.

KIPPER CAKES

Cooking time about 15 minutes
Serves 4

METRIC/IMPERIAL

225 g/8 oz cooked kipper fillets
225 g/8 oz mashed potato
25 g/1 oz butter
1 beaten egg
1 teaspoon chopped parsley
salt and pepper

for coating
1 beaten egg
2 tablespoons browned
   breadcrumbs
for frying
fat

In a large bowl mix together flaked kipper, mashed potato, softened butter, beaten egg and parsley. Season well with a little salt and with pepper. Divide mixture into four and mould into round cakes.

Dip the cakes into egg and then in breadcrumbs. Fry in hot fat on both sides until golden brown. Drain on crumpled kitchen paper and serve at once.

BAKED BUTTERED BLOATERS

Cooking time 10 minutes
Oven temperature Moderate
180°C, 350°F, Gas Mark 4
Serves 4

METRIC/IMPERIAL

4 bloaters
50 g/2 oz butter
2 tablespoons lemon juice

salt and pepper
4 slices buttered toast

Cut off heads, tails and fins and bone bloaters. Put in a greased oven-proof dish, dot with butter and season well with lemon juice, salt and pepper. Cover and bake for 10 minutes in a moderate oven. Pile on hot buttered toast.

HERRINGS IN ALE

Cooking time   1–1½ hours
Oven temperature   Cool
140°C, 275°F, Gas Mark 1
Serves 4

METRIC/IMPERIAL

4–6 herrings
salt and pepper
about 300 ml/½ pint ale

2 teaspoons mixed pickling
  spice
4 bay leaves
2 small onions

Clean, split and fillet the herrings. Season well with salt and pepper.
Roll them up, skin inwards, beginning at the tail. Place them neatly
and fairly close together in an ovenproof dish. Cover with the ale and
sprinkle with mixed pickling spice. Garnish with bay leaves and rings
of onion. Bake in a cool oven.

Note If liked, 15 g/½ oz powdered aspic jelly can be added to the
liquid after cooking. Allow herrings to cool in the liquid as it sets.

HERRINGS WITH RED CABBAGE

Cooking time   2 hour 10 minutes
Oven temperature   Moderate
180°C, 350°F, Gas Mark 4
Serves 4

METRIC/IMPERIAL

25 g/1 oz butter
2 medium onions, chopped
675 g/1½ lb red cabbage, finely
  shredded
75 g/3 oz soft brown sugar

4 tablespoons wine vinegar
salt and pepper
4 herrings
for garnish
lemon slices

Melt the butter in a pan or in a flameproof casserole. Add the onion
and fry for about 5 minutes until soft and golden. Add red cabbage
and cook for a further 5 minutes. Stir in sugar and vinegar. Season
with salt and pepper. If in a pan, transfer at this stage to an ovenproof
casserole. Cover. Bake in a moderate oven for 2 hours, or until tender.

Clean herrings and place them on top of the red cabbage for the
last 20 minutes of the cooking time. Garnish with lemon slices.

CRAB SALADS

Serves 4

METRIC/IMPERIAL

225 g/8 oz cooked crab meat   1 lettuce
2 hard-boiled eggs   *for garnish*
¼ cucumber   watercress sprigs
3 tablespoons mayonnaise
   (see page 30)

Flake the crab and mix with chopped eggs and diced cucumber in a bowl. Bind together with the mayonnaise. Place a bed of shredded lettuce on each of four scallop shells. Divide crab mixture between the shells and garnish with watercress. Serve with thinly sliced brown bread and butter.

LOBSTER MAYONNAISE

Serves 4

METRIC/IMPERIAL

2 medium cooked lobsters   sliced tomatoes
150 ml/¼ pint mayonnaise (see   sliced cucumber
   page 30)   watercress
1 lettuce

Split each lobster with a sharp knife down the centre. Open the halves, cut-side uppermost. Remove and discard intestine (long black line running to tail). Discard lady fingers (found where small claws join the body). Carefully remove stomach bag, situated near the head. Reserve bright pink coral for garnish. Remove the large claws, then crack with a weight. Take out the flesh from the claws in one piece if possible and add to the other flesh scooped out from the body of the lobster.

Mix lobster meat with mayonnaise, then pile back into the shells and decorate with coral. Serve on a bed of lettuce with tomato and cucumber slices and watercress.

SEAFOOD PLATTER

Serves 4

METRIC/IMPERIAL

225 g/8 oz cooked crab meat
600 ml/1 pint peeled prawns
175 g/6 oz button mushrooms, sliced
175 g/6 oz cold cooked rice
300 ml/½ pint double cream
1 tablespoon mayonnaise (see page 30)
1 teaspoon grated onion
a little grated horseradish
salt and pepper
1 tablespoon chopped chives

Mix the flaked crab with prawns, mushrooms and rice in a bowl. Whip the cream, add mayonnaise, onion and horseradish to taste. Add cream sauce to fish mixture and blend well together. Season to taste. Turn into a serving dish and sprinkle with chopped chives.

Meat and Poultry Dinners

It has been said that traditional British cooking has remained simple because meat and poultry, though not always cheap, have usually been plentiful. A roast sirloin or a fat capon needs no artifice – they make excellent meals in their own right.

The country housewife has always excelled at cooking the prime cuts of meat, but her proper sense of thrift has helped her to devise tasty stews, meat puddings and pies. These recipes are of particular interest now that meat is a major item in the budget, and I've included a selection in the recipes that follow. Here are some tips on the care and cooking of meat to help you make the most of this valuable food.

Uncooked meat stored in the larder should be wrapped in muslin and hung from a meat hook, or put on a plate and covered in muslin to protect it from flies.

Uncooked meat stored in the refrigerator should be put in the chiller tray, immediately under the freezer, or on a plate with kitchen foil lying loosely on top. Never put it in a sealed container.

Keep cooked meat which is to be eaten cold in the same way as raw meat in the larder. In the refrigerator, wrap it in kitchen foil; remove 30 minutes before serving.

Raw minced meat should be used up the day it is minced.

Offal should not be hung, but eaten as soon as possible after buying.

Frozen and chilled meat should be thoroughly defrosted before cooking.

Coarse and cheap cuts of meat are equal in food value to prime cuts, but need longer, slower cooking to make them really tender.

Use the residue in the tin or pan after roasting or frying meat as a basis for gravy – these juices are good for you.

If the meat includes the bone, use it to make stock as a basis for soups.

All offal, especially liver, is very nutritious. Try to include it regularly in your diet.

Roasting times—don't over-cook and dry up meat when roasting. Weigh your joint and calculate the cooking time according to the recipe before putting it in the oven.

When frying place meat in hot, shallow fat; this seals in the juices.

Don't use too much liquid in stews and casseroles.

Pre-heat grill before grilling meat, to seal in juices.

Poultry, once a luxury, is now within the reach of the average purse. If you are using the frozen variety, do give it time to thaw out at room temperature before cooking.

Meat Dishes

ROAST BEEF AND YORKSHIRE PUDDING

Cooking time   about 1¼ hours
Oven temperature   Moderately hot
200°C, 400°F, Gas Mark 6, then hot 220°C, 425°F, Gas Mark 7
Serves 4

METRIC/IMPERIAL

about 1.5 kg/3 lb sirloin beef, boned and rolled	large pinch salt
	1 egg
75 g/3 oz dripping or lard	300 ml/½ pint milk
for Yorkshire pudding	
110 g/4 oz self-raising or plain flour	

Place weighed joint in a roasting tin and add dripping. Place in a hot oven and roast, allowing 25 minutes per half kilo/per lb.

Sift flour and salt into a bowl. Add egg, then gradually add half the milk, stirring the flour from sides of the bowl using a wooden spoon. Beat well until the mixture is smooth. Gently stir in the rest of the milk. 40 minutes before joint is done increase oven heat to hot, 220°C, 425°F, Gas Mark 7. Remove joint from the roasting tin and pour off excess fat. Put a trivet in the centre of the pan and quickly pour in the batter. Place joint on the trivet and return to the oven as near the top as possible.

Serve as soon as Yorkshire pudding is well risen, crisp and golden brown.

BRAISED BEEF IN CIDER

Cooking time 1¾–2¼ *hours*
Oven temperature *Moderately hot*
190°C, 375°F, Gas Mark 5
Serves 4

450 g/1 lb topside beef, cut into
    thin slices
seasoned flour
40 g/1½ oz dripping
225 g/8 oz onions, sliced

1 bay leaf
1 sprig thyme
salt and pepper
300 ml/½ pint dry cider

Beat slices of meat with a rolling pin until they are very thin, and coat with seasoned flour. Melt the dripping in a frying pan and fry meat for few minutes until browned on both sides. Place in a casserole.

Gently fry the onions until soft and add to casserole with herbs and seasoning. Pour the cider over. Cover with the lid and cook in a moderately hot oven for 1½–2 hours or until meat is tender; add more cider, if necessary, during cooking.

CASSEROLE OF BEEF

Cooking time 3–3¼ *hours*
Oven temperature *Moderate*
160°C, 325°F, Gas Mark 3
Serves 4

40 g/1½ oz cooking fat
2 large onions, peeled and sliced
675 g/1½ lb stewing steak
40 g/1½ oz plain flour
1 teaspoon curry powder

600 ml/1 pint beef stock
2 tablespoons tomato purée
450 g/1 lb carrots, peeled and
    sliced
salt and pepper

Melt the fat in a pan and fry onions until tender, about 5 minutes. Trim and cut the meat into cubes, add to the pan and fry quickly until brown all over. Mix in the flour and curry powder, then blend in the stock, tomato purée, carrots and seasoning to taste.

Bring to the boil, transfer to a casserole, cover and place in a moderate oven for 2¾–3¼ hours. Serve with boiled potatoes.

STEAK AND KIDNEY PIE

Cooking time   2⅜ hours
Oven temperature   Moderately hot
200°C, 400°F, Gas Mark 6
Serves 4

METRIC/IMPERIAL

225 g/8 oz short crust or flaky
  pastry (see page 69)
for filling
450 g/1 lb stewing steak
225 g/8 oz sheep's kidneys
25 g/1 oz dripping

1 small onion, chopped
1 tablespoon plain flour
300 ml/½ pint stock
salt and pepper
for glaze
beaten egg

Trim and cut the steak into cubes. Skin, core and chop kidneys. Melt dripping in a pan, add onion, steak and kidneys and toss in hot fat until lightly browned. Stir in the flour, mix well, then add the stock. Season to taste, bring to the boil, reduce heat and simmer about 1¾ hours or until tender. Place in a 1-litre/1½-pint pie dish, allow to cool.

Damp edges of pie dish and cover with rolled-out pastry. Rough up edges and flute. Make pastry leaves with trimmings and damp before putting on pastry. Brush top of the pie with beaten egg.

Bake in moderately hot oven for about 45 minutes or until golden.

STEAK, KIDNEY AND MUSHROOM PUDDING

Cooking time   4 hours
Serves 4

METRIC/IMPERIAL

225 g/8 oz suet crust pastry (see
  page 71)
for filling
450 g/1 lb lean stewing steak
100 g/4 oz ox kidney

100 g/4 oz mushrooms
1 tablespoon plain flour
½ teaspoon salt
¼ teaspoon ground pepper
about 6 tablespoons stock or water

Trim and cut the meat into small neat pieces. Skin, core and roughly chop kidney. Wipe and slice the mushrooms. Toss the meats and mushrooms in flour, salt and pepper. Line a greased pudding basin with most of the rolled-out pastry, retaining just enough for the cover.

Place prepared meats and mushrooms in basin, then pour in stock or water nearly to cover. Damp edges of the pastry. Roll out rest of the pastry for a lid, place in position and press edges firmly together to seal. Use a sharp knife to trim edges neatly. Cover top closely with aluminium foil.

Place in the top of a steamer and steam steadily for about 4 hours, refilling bottom pan with boiling water as necessary. Remove foil from pudding. Arrange a clean napkin round the basin for holding and to serve.

BOILED BEEF AND DUMPLINGS

Cooking time   about 2½ hours
Serves 4

METRIC/IMPERIAL

900 g/2 lb salt silverside or topside	450 g/1 lb carrots, peeled and quartered
cold water to cover	*for dumplings*
bouquet garni (parsley, thyme, bay leaf, tied together)	110 g/4 oz self-raising flour
	1 teaspoon salt
4 onions, peeled and stuck with cloves	50 g/2 oz shredded suet
	cold water to mix

Put the meat into a pan with sufficient cold water to cover, bring slowly to boiling point and skim. Reduce heat to simmering point. Add the bouquet garni and the onions. Allow to simmer for about 1¼ hours, then remove bouquet garni. Add carrots and continue to simmer for a further 45 minutes, or until vegetables are just tender.

Meanwhile, sift flour with salt and add suet. Mix lightly with cold water to make a fairly soft dough. Divide into about eight pieces and with floured hands, form into balls. Add to meat and vegetables when vegetables are tender, and continue to simmer for another 15–20 minutes.

Serve the meat on a hot dish with the vegetables and dumplings arranged round, a little of the liquor poured on to the dish, and more handed separately in a sauce boat.

STEAK IN BEER AND MUSHROOM SAUCE

Cooking time   30 minutes
Serves 4

METRIC/IMPERIAL

675 g/1½ lb rump steak
1 clove garlic
4 tablespoons vegetable oil
for sauce
50 g/2 oz butter
225 g/8 oz mushrooms, sliced

2 teaspoons cornflour
300 ml/½ pint beer
salt and pepper
1 teaspoon tomato purée
1 teaspoon Worcestershire sauce

Buy the steak cut in one thick slice; cut into good sized cubes. Crush the garlic and simmer this gently in oil in a frying pan. Add the steak and cook gently until sealed and tender, 20 minutes.

Meanwhile, in a saucepan heat the butter and lightly fry mushrooms for about 4 minutes. Blend cornflour with a little of the beer and add to mushrooms, cook for a minute or two, stirring, then add the rest of the beer. Season and bring to the boil. Add tomato purée and Worcestershire sauce, cook for a minute or two, stirring. Turn steak on to a hot serving plate and pour over it the mushroom and beer sauce.

PORK 'N' PARSNIPS

Cooking time   1½ hours
Oven temperature   Moderately hot
200°C, 400°F, Gas Mark 6
Serves 4

METRIC/IMPERIAL

450 g/1 lb potatoes
450 g/1 lb parsnips
675 g/1½ lb belly pork, with skin
   scored

salt and pepper
1 tablespoon redcurrant jelly

Peel and halve the potatoes and parsnips. Boil in salted water for 2 minutes. Strain and reserve the liquid. Rub the skin of the pork with salt and pepper. Put in a roasting pan with the potatoes and parsnips round it. Add one teacup of the liquid.

Dissolve the redcurrant jelly in another 2 tablespoons of the liquid

and pour it over the pork. Cook in a moderately hot oven for about
1½ hours.

RAISED PORK AND APPLE PIE

Cooking time 2–2½ hours
Oven temperature Moderate
180°C, 350°F, Gas Mark 4
Serves 4–6

METRIC/IMPERIAL

350 g/12 oz hot water crust
  pastry (see below)
for filling
1 kg/2 lb pork fillet, diced
1 apple, peeled, cored and
  shredded

salt and pepper
7 tablespoons stock or water
1 beaten egg
1 teaspoon powdered gelatine
½ teaspoon meat extract

Line a greased and floured raised pie mould with two-thirds of
rolled-out pastry. Arrange layers of pork and apple in mould, seasoning each layer with salt and pepper.

Pour in 3 tablespoons stock or water. Damp pastry edges and cover
with remaining rolled-out pastry; decorate with leaves made from
pastry trimmings. Make an air vent in centre, and brush with beaten
egg. Bake in centre of a moderate oven for 2–2½ hours. After 1¾
hours, if pastry is firm, remove mould and brush sides with beaten
egg.

Leave the cooked pie to cool. Melt gelatine in remaining stock or
water, stir in meat extract and allow to cool and partially set. Pour
setting gelatine mixture into the pie through hole in the centre, and
leave to set before serving.

HOT WATER CRUST PASTRY FOR RAISED PIES

Makes 350 g/12 oz hot water pie crust

METRIC/IMPERIAL

350 g/12 oz plain flour
pinch salt

110 g/4 oz lard
150 ml/¼ pint water

Sift the flour and salt into a basin. Melt the fat in warm water and
add to flour. Mix with a knife and knead gently with the fingers.
Use while still warm.

POACHER'S ROLL

Cooking time   45 minutes
Oven temperature   Moderately hot
190°C, 375°F, Gas Mark 5
Serves 4

METRIC/IMPERIAL

350 g/12 oz short crust pastry
   (see page 69)
for filling
450 g/1 lb pork sausage meat
1 cooking apple, peeled, cored
   and grated

1 (198-g/7-oz) can sweetcorn
   kernels
1 teaspoon chopped fresh or
   dried tarragon
salt and pepper
for glaze
beaten egg

Roll out pastry on lightly floured board into an oblong about 25 by 28 cm/10 by 11 inches. Mix the filling together and spread over pastry to within 2 cm/1 inch of the edge. Brush round the edge with beaten egg and roll up pastry as for a sausage roll; place on baking tray. Brush roll with beaten egg and decorate with pastry circles cut from trimmings, brush these with beaten egg.

Bake in a moderately hot oven for about 45 minutes or until golden. Serve hot or cold, cut into slices.

DEVILLED PORK CHOPS

Cooking time   about 30 minutes
Serves 4

METRIC/IMPERIAL

4 lean pork chops
1 tablespoon bacon fat or
   dripping
75 g/3 oz butter or margarine
2 teaspoons dry mustard
2 teaspoons curry powder or
   paste

½ teaspoon ground ginger
½ teaspoon salt
1 tablespoon Worcestershire
   sauce
225 g/8 oz fresh white
   breadcrumbs

Trim the chops and fry in fat for 15–20 minutes, depending on thickness, until cooked. Meanwhile, cream butter or margarine with mustard, curry powder or paste, ginger, salt and sauce. When chops are cooked, allow to get cool, then smear the mixture well over the chops. Sprinkle with breadcrumbs and put under hot grill for a few minutes until breadcrumbs are golden brown.

LIVER AND BACON CASSEROLE

Cooking time   about 1¾ hours
Oven temperature   Moderate
180°C, 350°F, Gas Mark 4
Serves 4

METRIC/IMPERIAL

350 g/12 oz ox liver	100 g/4 oz streaky bacon
2 tablespoons plain flour	225 g/8 oz carrots
salt and pepper	300 ml/½ pint stock or water
50 g/2 oz lard or bacon dripping	450 g/1 lb potatoes
225 g/8 oz onions	

Wash, dry and cut the liver into slices. Coat with the flour, seasoned with salt and pepper. Melt the fat in a frying pan and fry the liver and peeled and sliced onions until brown. Transfer the liver and onions to a casserole. Add the trimmed bacon and peeled and sliced carrots. Mix any remaining flour into the fat in the frying pan and then blend in the stock or water and seasoning to taste and bring to the boil, still stirring. Pour into the casserole and cover.

Place in a moderate oven for 1½ hours. Add peeled and sliced potatoes halfway through the cooking time.

ROAST STUFFED LOIN OF LAMB

Cooking time   about 1½ hours
Oven temperature   Hot
220°C, 425°F, Gas Mark 7 for 15 minutes;
moderate 180°C, 350°F, Gas Mark 4 for 1¼ hours
Serves 4–6

METRIC/IMPERIAL

about 1.5 kg/3 lb boned loin lamb

little dripping

for stuffing

75 g/3 oz fresh white breadcrumbs

40 g/1½ oz shredded suet

½ teaspoon mixed herbs

grated rind of ½ lemon

salt and pepper

beaten egg

Mix the breadcrumbs with suet, herbs, lemon rind and seasoning. Add sufficient beaten egg to mix to a stiff consistency. Put stuffing neatly where the bone was removed from joint. Roll up and tie in several places with fine string. Weigh joint and calculate cooking time, allowing 20 minutes to the half kilo/lb and 20 minutes over.

Put the stuffed joint in a roasting tin, dot with dripping and roast in a hot oven for the first 15 minutes; reduce heat to moderate for rest of cooking time and baste now and then.

LAMB CASSEROLE WITH CRUSTY TOPPING

Cooking time   2 hours 35 minutes
Oven temperature   Moderate
160°C, 325°F, Gas Mark 3 for 2 hours;
moderately hot 190°C, 375°F, Gas Mark 5 for 20 minutes
Serves 4–6

METRIC/IMPERIAL

900 g/2 lb lamb shoulder, neck or breast

25 g/1 oz well-seasoned flour

25 g/1 oz cooking fat, lard or dripping

2 medium onions, peeled and thinly sliced

3 sticks celery, chopped

600 ml/1 pint water

2 tablespoons tomato purée

¼ teaspoon salt

4 slices bread, well buttered

Divide the meat into 3-cm/1-inch pieces and coat with seasoned flour. Melt the fat in a pan, add vegetables and fry over medium heat until light golden. Move to one side and fry the meat. Transfer to a casserole dish, then pour over it the water mixed with the tomato purée and salt. Cover with a lid and cook in a moderate oven for 2 hours.

Remove casserole from the oven. Cut each slice of bread into four triangles and arrange on top of the meat, buttered side up. Return to a moderately hot oven for 20 minutes until bread is golden brown.

SAVOURY BAKED VEAL

Cooking time   about 1½ hours
Oven temperature   Moderately hot
190°C, 375°F, Gas Mark 5
Serves 4–6

METRIC/IMPERIAL

1.5 kg/3 lb boned leg veal, the fillet end	1 tablespoon dry mustard
1 teaspoon chopped sage	1 teaspoon salt
1 teaspoon brown sugar	3 tablespoons tarragon vinegar
	4 rashers bacon

Ask the butcher to tie boned joint into a neat shape for roasting. Put the meat, skin side up, in a deep casserole. Mix sage, sugar, mustard, salt and vinegar together. Pour it over the meat. Remove rinds and put bacon on top of meat. Cover with lid or aluminium foil.

Bake in a moderately hot oven for about 1½ hours or until tender, basting from time to time. Remove string before serving. Serve hot or cold, sliced thinly.

Poultry Dishes

DUCKLING CASSEROLE

Cooking time   about 2–2½ hours
Oven temperature   Moderate
180°C, 350°F, Gas Mark 4 for 15 minutes;
cool 150°C, 300°F, Gas Mark 2 for 1½–2 hours
Serves 4

METRIC/IMPERIAL

1 duckling cut into four portions	150 ml/¼ pint stock
salt and black pepper	1 carrot
2 onions	2 sticks celery
1 bay leaf	100 g/4 oz button mushrooms
300 ml/½ pint red wine	grated orange rind
100 g/4 oz bacon	chopped parsley
a little cooking oil	

Wipe the duckling with a damp cloth, sprinkle with salt and freshly ground black pepper. Peel, slice and chop onions, and place in a bowl with seasoned duckling and bay leaf. Pour wine over it and leave to stand in a cool place for 2 hours. Remove the portions with a draining spoon; dry on absorbent paper. Reserve liquid.

Trim the bacon, cut into pieces and cook in the oil gently for 3–4 minutes. Add duckling and brown all over in hot oil. Drain the duckling well, then place in an ovenproof casserole and cook in a moderate oven for 15 minutes. Remove from the oven, pour over it the wine mixture and prepared stock. Peel and chop carrot, chop celery and rinse mushrooms; add to casserole. Cover and return to cool oven for a further 1½–2 hours or until tender. Remove excess fat with soft kitchen paper. Sprinkle with orange rind and parsley.

ROAST DUCKLING WITH APPLE AND ORANGE SAUCE

Cooking time   about 1 hour 40 minutes
Oven temperature   Moderate
180°C, 350°F, Gas Mark 4
Serves 4

METRIC/IMPERIAL

1 dressed duckling, about
   1.75 kg/4 lb
salt and pepper
for sauce
225 g/8 oz cooking apples
finely grated rind and juice of
   1 large orange
25 g/1 oz butter
1 tablespoon demerara sugar

for gravy
duckling giblets
salt and pepper
bay leaf
3 tablespoons plain flour
3 tablespoons water
1 teaspoon vegetable extract
1 tablespoon chopped parsley

Sprinkle duckling with salt and pepper. Place in a roasting pan and prick the skin well with a fork, cook in a moderate oven allowing 20 minutes per half kilo/per lb plus 20 minutes. Baste frequently. Garnish with slices of orange and watercress. Hand sauce and gravy separately.

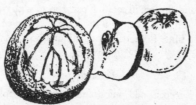

To prepare apple and orange sauce

Peel apples, grate on coarse grater. Mix with orange rind and juice. Place butter in small saucepan, heat gently until just melted. Add apple and orange mixture and stir over gentle heat until smooth. Beat in sugar just before serving.

To prepare gravy

Cover duckling giblets with water. Season with salt and pepper, add bay leaf. Simmer for 1 hour. Blend flour, water, vegetable extract and parsley in small saucepan. Gradually blend in strained hot stock and cook, over gentle heat, stirring, for a few minutes. Season if necessary.

ROAST CHICKEN WITH COUNTRY STUFFING

Cooking time   about 1½ hours
Oven temperature   Moderately hot
190°C, 375°F, Gas Mark 5
Serves 4

METRIC/IMPERIAL

1 dressed chicken, about 1.5 kg/3 lb	1 tablespoon chopped parsley
50 g/2 oz butter	salt and pepper
for stuffing	beaten egg to bind
50 g/2 oz butter	*for gravy*
1 onion, chopped	sediment left in roasting pan
2 celery sticks, chopped	1 tablespoon plain flour
100 g/4 oz fresh white breadcrumbs	600 ml/1 pint chicken stock, made from giblets
finely grated rind of 1 lemon	salt and pepper

Prepare stuffing and stuff chicken. Weigh chicken and calculate the cooking time, allowing 20 minutes per half kilo/per lb and 20 minutes over. Stand chicken in roasting pan, spread with butter and cover with aluminium foil. Roast in a moderately hot oven for the calculated cooking time. Remove foil 15 minutes before end to allow for browning.

For stuffing

Melt fat in saucepan, add onion and celery and cook gently for 5 minutes. Mix in breadcrumbs, lemon rind and parsley. Season to taste and bind with egg.

For gravy

Pour off fat from roasting pan leaving sediment and juices; blend in flour and cook for 2 or 3 minutes. Add stock gradually, stirring until smooth. Season to taste.

Cooking time   15 minutes
Serves 4

METRIC/IMPERIAL

25 g/1 oz butter

25 g/1 oz flour

200 ml/⅓ pint milk

225 g/8 oz cooked chicken, finely chopped

225 g/8 oz ham, finely chopped

2 small red-skinned apples, cored and chopped

grated rind of 1 lemon

salt and pepper

for coating and frying

beaten egg

breadcrumbs

fat for deep frying

for garnish

parsley

Make a thick white sauce with the butter, flour and milk. Add the finely chopped meats, apple and lemon rind. Season to taste. Allow mixture to cool. Form into cork shapes, dust with flour and coat with beaten egg and breadcrumbs. Chill for 45 minutes. Deep fry about 10 minutes until golden. Drain on kitchen paper. Serve garnished with parsley.

CRISP FRIED CHICKEN WITH PIQUANT BROWN SAUCE

Cooking time   about 50 minutes
Serves 4

METRIC/IMPERIAL

4 chicken joints	*for piquant brown sauce*
50 g/2 oz flour	25 g/1 oz butter or bacon
1½ teaspoons dry mustard	dripping
1 teaspoon salt	25 g/1 oz flour
¼ teaspoon freshly ground pepper	1 teaspoon made mustard
50 g/2 oz butter	1 teaspoon Worcestershire sauce
50 g/2 oz bacon dripping	450 ml/¾ pint chicken stock
	salt and pepper

Coat chicken joints with seasoned flour, shaking one at a time in a paper bag. Melt butter and bacon fat and fry chicken joints slowly, turning to brown; cover and cook very gently for about 30 minutes. Uncover and cook for another 10 minutes, until crisp and brown.

Meanwhile, make sauce: melt fat in saucepan and blend in flour, cook, stirring until browned. Stir in mustard and Worcestershire sauce, then stock. Cook, stirring until thick and smooth. Season with salt and pepper.

DORSET RABBIT

Cooking time   2 hours 15 minutes
Oven temperature   Moderate
180°C, 350°F, Gas Mark 4
Serves 4

METRIC/IMPERIAL

1 young rabbit, jointed	100 g/4 oz shredded suet
1 tablespoon seasoned flour	2 large onions, finely chopped
4 rashers fat bacon, trimmed	2 teaspoons finely chopped or
2 tablespoons cider	powdered sage
for topping	grated rind of ½ small lemon
225 g/8 oz fresh white	1 beaten egg plus little milk
breadcrumbs	

Wash the rabbit and blanch (put in cold water, bring to the boil and drain), pat dry in a clean cloth and toss in seasoned flour. Lay joints in a casserole, cover with bacon and pour cider over them.

Mix topping ingredients together, adding sufficient milk to bind to a stuffing consistency. Cover rabbit with mixture, pressing down evenly with the hand. Cover and bake in a moderate oven for 2 hours. Remove lid and cook for about 15 minutes longer to brown topping.

RABBIT AND BACON PUDDING

Cooking time   4 hours
Serves 4

METRIC/IMPERIAL

225 g/8 oz suet crust pastry (see page 71)	225 g/8 oz lean bacon collar, soaked overnight
for filling	2 onions, chopped
350–450 g/12 oz–1 lb jointed rabbit	2 cooking apples, chopped
	salt and pepper
	cider or stock

Wash the rabbit and blanch (bring to the boil in cold water and drain). Cut the bacon into cubes. Line a greased pudding basin with most of rolled-out pastry, retaining just enough for the cover. Fill with layers of rabbit, bacon, onion and apple, seasoning each layer. Pour in cider or stock nearly to cover. Damp edges of pastry. Roll our rest of the pastry for a lid and place in position; press edges firmly together to seal. Use a sharp knife to trim edges neatly. Cover top closely with aluminium foil leaving room for pudding to swell.

Place in top of a steamer and steam steadily for 4 hours, refilling bottom pan as necessary. Remove foil from the pudding. Arrange a clean napkin round the bowl for holding, and serve.

Puddings and Pies

Britain's unique contribution to European cookery is, without doubt, a flair for producing delicious puddings and pies. Give a Frenchman, an Italian or any other Continental a real home-baked apple pie with a dollop of fresh cream and he'll rave about it.

Many of us nurture a secret longing for those massive puddings that for generations have kept our climate at bay: apple dumplings, spotted dog, and all those wonderful puddings and pies which are so typically British.

Here are a few tips to help you make *really light pastry:*

Weigh and measure ingredients carefully; it's most important to use the correct proportion of fat to flour.

Use plain flour, except in suet crust, and sift with salt into a good sized mixing bowl. Have the fat at room temperature. It must be firm but pliable; in no case allow it to 'oil'.

Use fingertips only to rub the fat into the flour, never use the palm of the hand. And lift the mixture in the air each time to introduce as much air as possible.

Add the liquid carefully as the amount given in the recipe can only be a guide: it will vary with the type of flour and fat used. Too little water makes the pastry difficult to handle because of cracks, too much water makes it tough and hard when it is cooked.

Don't over-handle the dough. Roll briskly and firmly in one direction only, using only a little flour for dredging the board.

Bake pastry quickly in a moderately hot to hot oven.

Note When quantities of pastry are given in this book the amount indicates the weight of flour used in recipe; increase or decrease other ingredients accordingly. For example, for 110 g/4 oz pastry use 110 g/4 oz flour.

To bake blind

This prevents pastry rising during cooking when making flan, tart or pie cases. If making a flan, then stand the flan ring on a baking sheet first. Line the flan ring, tart or pie plate with rolled-out pastry, press down to fit, trim edge. Prick the base lightly with a fork. Line the inside with a square of greaseproof paper and weight it down with rice or dried beans. Bake in a moderately hot oven 190°C, 375°F, Gas Mark 5 for 15 minutes to set the pastry. Remove paper and rice or beans and return flan to oven for a further 10 minutes, or until cooked.

Note Rice or beans can be stored in a screw-top jar and used again.

Pastry Making

SHORT CRUST PASTRY

Makes 225 g/8 oz short crust pastry

METRIC/IMPERIAL

225 g/8 oz plain flour
pinch salt
50 g/2 oz butter or margarine

50 g/2 oz lard or cooking fat
about 3 tablespoons cold water

Sift the flour and salt into a bowl, add fats and cut into flour with a knife. Use fingertips to rub in fat lightly until mixture looks like fine breadcrumbs. Stir water in with a knife, then draw mixture together with fingers to form a firm but pliable dough. Knead gently on a lightly floured board until free from cracks.

FLAKY PASTRY

Makes 225 g/8 oz flaky pastry

METRIC/IMPERIAL

225 g/8 oz plain flour
pinch salt

175 g/6 oz butter or margarine
150 ml/¼ pint cold water

Sift the flour with salt into a bowl. Divide fat into three portions. Rub one portion of fat lightly into flour. Use sufficient cold water to mix to rolling consistency. Roll out dough to oblong shape. Take the second portion of fat, divide it into small pieces and lay them on the surface of two-thirds of the dough. Leave the remaining third without fat, take its two corners and fold back over second third so that the dough looks like an envelope with its flap open. Fold over top end of pastry, so closing the 'envelope'. Turn pastry at right angles, seal open ends of pastry and 'rib' it (this means gently depress it at intervals to give a corrugated effect); this distributes the air and helps pastry to rise evenly. Repeat the process again using the remaining fat and turning pastry in the same way. Roll out pastry once more, but should it begin to feel very soft and sticky put in a cold place for 30 minutes before rolling out.

Fold pastry as before, turn it, seal edges and rib it. Altogether the pastry should have three foldings and three turnings. It is then ready to stand in a cold place before using.

RICH SHORT CRUST PASTRY

Makes 225 g/8 oz rich short crust pastry

METRIC/IMPERIAL

225 g/8 oz plain flour
pinch salt
110 g/4 oz butter or margarine

1 egg yolk
1–1½ tablespoons cold water

Sift the flour with salt into a bowl, add fat and cut into flour with a knife. Use fingertips to rub in fat lightly until mixture looks like fine breadcrumbs. Mix the egg yolk with the water, tip into flour and fat mixture and work to a firm dough. Turn on to a lightly floured board and knead lightly until smooth.

Note For sweet dishes add 2 teaspoons castor sugar after rubbing fat into flour.

70

SUET CRUST PASTRY

Makes 225 g/8 oz suet crust pastry

METRIC/IMPERIAL

225 g/8 oz self-raising flour
pinch salt

110 g/4 oz shredded suet
cold water to mix

Sift the flour and salt into a bowl, mix in the suet. Add sufficient cold water to mix to a firm dough. Knead lightly on a floured board.

Pudding Recipes

QUEEN OF PUDDINGS

Cooking time   about 40 minutes
Oven temperature   Moderately hot
190°C, 375°F, Gas Mark 5 for 25–30 minutes;
moderate 180°C, 350°F, Gas Mark 4 for 10 minutes
Serves 4

METRIC/IMPERIAL

300 ml/½ pint milk
peeled rind of 1 small lemon
15 g/½ oz butter
25 g/1 oz castor sugar
50 g/2 oz fresh white breadcrumbs
2 egg yolks

2–3 tablespoons strawberry or
    raspberry jam
for meringue topping
2 egg whites
100 g/4 oz castor sugar

Heat the milk very gently with the lemon rind, then leave in the covered pan for few minutes. Strain into a bowl, add the butter and sugar and, when dissolved, the breadcrumbs. Mix and leave to cool. Stir in the egg yolks, mix well together and turn into a lightly greased pie dish. Stand 30 minutes, then bake in a moderately hot oven for 25–30 minutes until set. Remove from oven, cool slightly; spread the top with jam.

Whisk egg whites until very stiff, add 2 teaspoons of sugar and whisk until satiny-looking; fold in rest of sugar. Pile meringue on top and put back in a moderate oven for 10 minutes until lightly browned.

CREAMY RICE PUDDING

Cooking time 2–3 hours
Oven temperature Cool
150°C, 300°F, Gas Mark 2
Serves 4

METRIC/IMPERIAL

40 g/1½ oz short-grain rice	600 ml/1 pint milk
40 g/1½ oz sugar	15 g/½ oz butter

Wash the rice in cold water. Put in a greased pie dish with the other ingredients. Stir well. Cook low down in a cool oven for 2 or 3 hours. After about 30 minutes you can stir in the skin; this helps to make an extra-creamy pudding.

MARMALADE SUET PUDDING

Cooking time 2–2½ hours
Serves 4

METRIC/IMPERIAL

110 g/4 oz plain flour	2–3 tablespoons marmalade
½ teaspoon salt	1 egg
2 teaspoons baking powder or 1 teaspoon bicarbonate of soda	150 ml/¼ pint milk
	for sauce
	3 tablespoons marmalade
110 g/4 oz fresh white breadcrumbs	3 tablespoons sugar
110 g/4 oz shredded suet	150 ml/¼ pint water
110 g/4 oz sugar	grated rind and juice of ½ lemon

Grease a 1-litre/1½-pint pudding basin. Sift the flour, salt and baking powder into a basin and add breadcrumbs, shredded suet, sugar and marmalade. Beat the egg and add milk to it. Add the egg and milk to the mixture. Mix with a wooden spoon until well blended and a soft consistency. Two-thirds fill the greased basin. Cover with greased greaseproof paper or aluminium foil. Steam for 2–2½ hours. Turn out on a serving dish.

For sauce

Put all the ingredients into a saucepan and heat, stirring until sugar is dissolved.

CASTLE PUDDINGS

Cooking time   15 minutes
Oven temperature   Moderately hot
190°C, 375°F, Gas Mark 5
Serves 4

METRIC/IMPERIAL

110 g/4 oz butter or margarine	*for jam sauce*
110 g/4 oz castor sugar	4 tablespoons raspberry jam
2 eggs	heated with 1 tablespoon
110 g/4 oz self-raising flour	water

Well grease eight dariole moulds. Cream the fat and sugar together until soft and fluffy. Beat in eggs, one at a time. Fold in the sifted flour. Half fill prepared moulds and place on a baking sheet. Bake in a moderately hot oven for 15 minutes, or until golden brown. Turn out on a hot dish and serve with jam sauce.

OLD-FASHIONED BREAD PUDDING

Cooking time   1½ hours
Oven temperature   Moderately hot
190°C, 375°F, Gas Mark 5
Serves 4

METRIC/IMPERIAL

9–10 slices stale bread	4 teaspoons mixed spice
150 g/5 oz mixed dried fruit	50 g/2 oz soft butter or
25 g/1 oz mixed peel	margarine
75 g/3 oz soft brown sugar	castor sugar for sprinkling

Grease an 18-cm/7-inch round cake tin or 15-cm/6-inch square tin or ovenproof dish. Soak the bread in cold water for at least 30 minutes. Squeeze the bread by hand or in a sieve to expel as much water as possible, then beat with a fork to remove any lumps. Add the remaining ingredients and mix thoroughly. Put the mixture into the greased tin or dish and bake in a moderately hot oven for about 1½ hours.

Sprinkle liberally with castor sugar and serve hot with custard, or cold with cream.

BROWN BETTY PUDDING

Cooking time 1–1½ hours
Oven temperature Moderate
160°C, 325°F, Gas Mark 3
Serves 4

METRIC/IMPERIAL

175 g/6 oz fine white breadcrumbs	1 lemon
900 g/2 lb cooking apples, peeled, cored and sliced	4 tablespoons golden syrup
	100 g/4 oz demerara sugar
	150 ml/¼ pint water

Grease a 1-litre/2-pint pie dish or casserole and coat it with a layer of breadcrumbs. Fill the pie dish with alternate layers of apples, grated lemon rind and breadcrumbs. Heat the syrup, sugar and water in a pan, add the lemon juice and pour them over the mixture. Bake in a moderate oven for 1–1½ hours until browned.

SPOTTED DICK

Cooking time 2–2½ hours
Serves 4

METRIC/IMPERIAL

225 g/8 oz plain flour	milk or milk and water to mix
2 teaspoons baking powder	*to serve*
50 g/2 oz sugar	brown sugar
75 g/3 oz shredded suet	custard
100 g/4 oz currants	

Mix together the flour, baking powder and sugar. Add the shredded suet and cleaned currants and mix with milk to a medium stiff dough, not too soft. Shape into a roll on a board, wrap a strip of greased paper round it, tie in a cloth like a sausage, leaving room for expansion. Boil for 2–2½ hours. Remove paper and cloth. Serve with brown sugar and custard.

BREAD AND BUTTER PUDDING

Cooking time   30–40 minutes
Oven temperature   Moderate
180°C, 350°F, Gas Mark 4
Serves 4

METRIC/IMPERIAL

4 or 5 small slices bread and
   butter, with crusts removed
40 g/1½ oz cleaned currants

1 egg
15 g/½ oz castor sugar
300 ml/½ pint milk

Cut the buttered bread into small pieces and place in a greased pie dish with currants sprinkled between the layers. Beat the egg, sugar and milk together with a fork and pour over the bread. Leave to stand for 15 minutes. Bake in a moderate oven for 30–40 minutes.

JUNKET

Cooking time   5 minutes
Serves 4

METRIC/IMPERIAL

600 ml/1 pint milk
2 teaspoons castor sugar

2 teaspoons essence rennet

Put the milk into a saucepan with the castor sugar and stir it over a gentle heat until it is at blood heat. Pour the milk into a deep dish or bowl and thoroughly stir in the rennet. Leave it to set in a warm place – it will take only a few minutes.

Serve with stewed fruit and cream.

FRUIT FOOL

Cooking time   25 minutes
Serves 4

METRIC/IMPERIAL

450 g/1 lb fruit (gooseberries,
   raspberries, etc.)
150 ml/¼ pint water (optional)
100 g/4 oz castor sugar

150 ml/¼ pint double cream
150 ml/¼ pint cold custard (same
   consistency as the cream)
ratafia biscuits

Stew the fruit gently with the water, if used, and sugar. Sieve finely and leave to cool. Whip the double cream until thick and put a little aside for decoration. Fold into the custard. Stir in the cold sieved fruit. Put into individual dishes and chill well.

Decorate with remaining cream and serve with ratafia biscuits.

FRUIT SPONGE CUPS

Cooking time   about 30 minutes
Serves 6

METRIC/IMPERIAL

175 g/6 oz self-raising flour	2 eggs
pinch salt	2 tablespoons milk
110 g/4 oz butter or margarine	110 g/4 oz blackcurrants or
150 g/5 oz castor sugar	redcurrants

Well grease six old tea cups or small moulds of just under 150-ml/ ¼-pint capacity, and put a circle of greased greaseproof paper in the bottom of each. Sift the flour and salt. Cream butter or margarine and 110 g/4 oz sugar together until light and fluffy. Beat in eggs gradually, adding 1 tablespoon flour with last amount of egg. Fold in remaining flour, and finally the milk. Mix remaining sugar with black- or redcurrants and place in bottom of cups or moulds.

Divide sponge mixture between cups on top of black- or redcurrants. Cover with greased foil or a double layer of greased greaseproof paper. Steam for about 30 minutes. Turn out and serve with whipped cream.

POOR KNIGHTS OF WINDSOR

Cooking time   10 minutes
Serves 4

METRIC / IMPERIAL

8 very thin slices bread	50 g/2 oz butter
2 eggs	jam or lemon juice
2 tablespoons milk	icing sugar
2 tablespoons sugar	*to serve*
½ teaspoon vanilla essence	whipped cream

Remove the crusts from the bread. Beat the eggs and pour on to a dinner plate, stir in the milk, sugar and vanilla essence and mix well together. Melt the butter in a frying pan and heat without browning. Dip the slices of bread into the egg mixture, just coating them on both sides, and fry on both sides until golden brown. Spread with jam and roll up. Secure with wooden cocktail sticks until set. Dust with icing sugar. Serve hot with whipped cream.

APPLE CHARLOTTE

Cooking time   50–60 minutes
Oven temperature   Moderate
180°C, 350°F, Gas Mark 4
Serves 4

METRIC/IMPERIAL

175 g/6 oz fine white breadcrumbs

110 g/4 oz shredded suet

50 g/2 oz granulated sugar *for fruit mixture*

40 g/1½ oz butter

2 tablespoons water

675 g/1½ lb cooking apples, peeled, cored and diced

75 g/3 oz brown sugar

25 g/1 oz sultanas or seedless raisins

¼ teaspoon cinnamon or mixed spice

Heavily grease a 1-litre/2-pint pie dish. Mix the breadcrumbs, suet and sugar well together, and press three-quarters of it on to bottom and sides of the dish.

Melt 25 g/1 oz butter in a pan, add the water and apples. Cover and heat gently, shaking and stirring occasionally, until apples are well glazed but not too soft. Remove from heat, stir in 50 g/2 oz brown sugar, sultanas and cinnamon. Pour into the prepared pie dish then top with remaining crumb mixture, pressing down neatly. Wipe edge of dish, then sprinkle crumbs with rest of brown sugar and dot with remaining butter. Bake in the centre of moderate oven for 50–60 minutes until golden brown.

OLD-FASHIONED CUSTARD TART

Cooking time   about 1 hour
Oven temperature   Moderately hot
190°C, 375°F, Gas Mark 5 for 30 minutes;
cool 150°C, 300°F, Gas Mark 2 for 30 minutes
Serves 4

METRIC/IMPERIAL

175 g/6 oz short crust pastry
(see page 69)

for filling

50–75 g/2–3 oz chopped mixed
peel

300 ml/½ pint milk, lukewarm

2 beaten eggs

25 g/1 oz castor sugar

powdered cinnamon

Roll pastry out on a lightly floured board to a 30-cm/12-inch round and use it to line a deep 23-cm/9-inch pie plate. Cover base evenly with peel. Pour milk over eggs and sugar and stir well. Strain into pastry-lined pie plate. Sprinkle top with cinnamon and bake for 30 minutes in a moderately hot oven, then in a cool oven for approximately a further 30 minutes, until pastry is golden and the custard set. Serve hot or cold.

BLACKBERRY AND APPLE TART

Cooking time 45–50 minutes
Oven temperature Hot
220°C, 425°F, Gas Mark 7 for 10 minutes;
moderate 180°C, 350°F, Gas Mark 4 for 35–40 minutes
Serves 4

METRIC/IMPERIAL

225 g/8 oz short crust pastry   225 g/8 oz blackberries
  (see page 69)   100 g/4 oz castor sugar
for filling   *for egg wash*
350 g/12 oz peeled, cored and   1 egg, beaten with 2 tablespoons
  thinly sliced cooking apples   water and 1 teaspoon sugar

Turn the pastry on to a floured board. Roll out two-thirds and with it line a 20-cm/8-inch pie plate. Fill with apples, blackberries and sugar to taste. Roll out rest of pastry, moisten edges and cover pie. Press edges well together to seal and decorate. Brush with egg wash. Bake towards top of a hot oven for 10 minutes, then in a moderate oven for 35–40 minutes.

APPLE PLATE PIE

Cooking time about 50 minutes
Oven temperature Moderately hot
200°C, 400°F, Gas Mark 6
Serves 4

METRIC/IMPERIAL

350 g/12 oz short crust pastry   225 g/8 oz granulated sugar
  (see page 69)   1 clove
for filling   *for glaze*
675 g/1½ lb cooking apples,   egg white or milk
  peeled, cored and sliced   castor sugar

Gently stew the apples with sugar, clove and very little water in a covered pan until tender, about 20 minutes. Allow to cool before using.

Roll out the pastry on a lightly floured board. Cut into two circles to fit a 23-cm/9-inch pie plate, making one circle slightly larger than the other. Lift the smaller circle on to pie plate, press down and put in prepared filling. Damp edges and cover with other circle. Seal edges, trim and flute. Make three small cuts across the centre. Brush top with egg white or milk and sprinkle with castor sugar. Stand pie on baking sheet and bake in a moderately hot oven for about 30 minutes.

APPLE DUMPLINGS

Cooking time   about 1 hour
Oven temperature   Hot
220°C, 425°F, Gas Mark 7 for 20 minutes;
moderately hot 190°C, 375°F, Gas Mark 5 for 40 minutes
Serves 4

METRIC / IMPERIAL

4 small cooking apples	450 g/1 lb short crust pastry
25 g/1 oz brown sugar	(see page 69)
15 g/½ oz dates or 4 cloves	egg beaten with a little water

Peel and core the apples and stuff the middles with the sugar and chopped dates or a clove. Roll out the pastry to 5-mm/¼-inch thickness, cut into four rounds large enough to enclose the apples. Place each apple in the centre of a pastry round, wet the edges and fold up round the apple, flattening the creases as much as possible. From trimmings form four plaits made by cutting three 5-mm/¼-inch wide strips, 15 cm/6 inches long, for each plait.

Brush dumplings with egg wash, place a plait over the top of each and brush again. Bake in a hot oven until the pastry has set and begins to brown (about 20 minutes', then reduce heat and continue to bake more slowly in a moderately hot oven, covering if necessary to prevent over-browning, until the apples are quite cooked (about 40 minutes).

RHUBARB AND ORANGE TART

Cooking time   about 30 minutes
Oven temperature   Moderately hot
200°C, 400°F, Gas Mark 6
Serves 4

METRIC/IMPERIAL

225 g/8 oz short crust pastry
(see page 69)
for filling
450 g/1 lb early rhubarb
175 g/6 oz sugar

25 g/1 oz flour
1 beaten egg
grated rind of 1 orange
2 tablespoons orange juice made
with water to 150 ml/¼ pint

Roll out the pastry on a lightly floured board and line a 20-cm/8-inch ovenproof plate, saving the trimmings for lattice. Wipe the rhubarb and cut into 3-cm/1-inch lengths and place in pastry case. In a basin blend together sugar, flour, egg and rind of orange. Place juice and water in a pan and bring to the boil. Pour on to flour mixture, stir briskly. Return to the pan and bring to the boil, stirring all the time. Pour over rhubarb. Cut strips from trimmings and place on filling to form a lattice.

Bake for about 30 minutes. Serve hot or cold.

ELIZABETHAN FLAN

Cooking time   about 55 minutes
Oven temperature   Moderately hot
190°C, 375°F, Gas Mark 5
Serves 4

METRIC/IMPERIAL

225 g/8 oz rich short crust
pastry (see page 70)
for filling
2 large thin-skinned oranges

2 tablespoons honey
150 ml/¼ pint water
150 ml/¼ pint double cream
50 g/2 oz granulated sugar

Wash the oranges and cut into thin rings; the peel should be kept on. Soak overnight in honey and water. Next day, place oranges and liquid in pan and simmer for 25–30 minutes. Drain and cool, reserve syrup. Stand a 20-cm/8-inch flan ring on a baking sheet and line with rolled-out pastry, trim edges. Bake blind (see page 68) in moderately hot oven for 15 minutes. Remove paper and filling and cook for further 10 minutes or until pale golden. Cool.

Whip cream until just stiff and spread over bottom of the flan case. Overlap orange slices on top. Add sugar to 150 ml/¼ pint honey liquid and heat gently until sugar has dissolved. Bring to boil and cook until syrupy consistency, 3–5 minutes. Use this to glaze oranges. Serve chilled.

FAVOURITE PLUM PIE

Cooking time   40 minutes
Oven temperature   Moderately hot
200°C, 400°F, Gas Mark 6
Serves 4

METRIC/IMPERIAL

350 g/12 oz short crust pastry (see page 69)	finely grated rind of 1 lemon
for filling	5 tablespoons water
900 g/2 lb plums	*for topping*
225 g/8 oz demerara sugar	castor sugar

Put washed fruit in a deep pie dish, sprinkle sugar and lemon rind between layers. Put a pie funnel in centre. Add water. Roll out pastry on lightly floured board into an oval slightly larger than pie top; cut a strip from the edge and use to line damped rim of pie dish; damp this strip and cover pie with rest of pastry. Trim, rough up and flute edges.

Make a small air vent in top. Stand pie on a baking sheet and cook in a moderately hot oven for about 40 minutes. Dredge the top with castor sugar.

PEAR PIE

Cooking time   about 30 minutes
Oven temperature   Moderately hot
200°C, 400°F, Gas Mark 6
Serves 4

METRIC/IMPERIAL

350 g/12 oz short crust pastry
  (see page 69)
for filling
900 g/2 lb medium ripe pears,
  peeled, cored and halved
juice of 1 lemon

piece cinnamon stick
3 tablespoons heated apricot jam
50 g/2 oz sugar
2 tablespoons water
for topping
castor sugar

Toss the pear halves lightly in lemon juice, leave to stand 10 minutes. Place pear halves in a deep pie dish, add cinnamon stick, apricot jam and sugar. Put a pie funnel in centre. Add water.

Roll out pastry on a lightly floured board into an oval, slightly larger than pie top, cut strip from edge and use to line damped rim of pie dish; damp this strip and cover pie with rest of pastry. Trim, rough up and flute edges. Make a small air vent in the top. Stand pie on a baking sheet and cook in a moderately hot oven for about 30 minutes. Dredge the top with castor sugar.

CREAMY PEAR FLAN

Cooking time   1 hour
Oven temperature   Moderately hot
190°C, 375°F, Gas Mark 5
Serves 4

METRIC/IMPERIAL

225 g/8 oz rich short crust pastry
  (see page 70)
for filling
3 small pears, peeled, cored and
  halved

150 ml/¼ pint double cream
50 g/2 oz sugar
1 teaspoon vanilla essence

Line a flan case with the pastry. Prick base with a fork and bake blind
(see page 68) for 10 minutes. Remove filling and cool slightly.

Arrange pears in base of the flan. Blend the cream, sugar and vanilla
essence and pour it over the pears. Bake in a moderately hot oven for
about 40 minutes. Serve hot or cold.

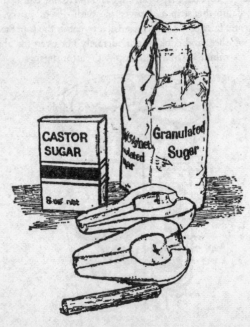

Farmhouse Bread and Tea Bakes

For those of us who have country memories there is one that is especially evocative: the wonderful warm and welcoming smell of baking. In this country, a special pride is still taken in the craft and there is no lack of competition to display cakes and bakes at local fêtes.

Baking bread is a particularly satisfying and rewarding task and the recipes I've included are not difficult to make.

If you find it difficult to buy fresh yeast, then dried yeast is an excellent substitute; sold in tins of various sizes it keeps well for up to six months in a cool place.

After the dough has been kneaded it is put to rise, which means left on one side until it swells and doubles its size. For a quick rise leave it in a warm place for 45–60 minutes, for a slower rise leave it for 2 hours at average room temperature.

It is then shaped into loaves and put to prove, or allowed to rise again, for about 20–30 minutes. Be careful not to over-prove the mixture or you'll lose the shape of the dough. Bake the bread in a very hot oven until deep golden brown and crusty – when it's cooked, the bread should sound hollow if you tap the base with your knuckles. Bread takes a short time to mix and a long time to rise, so organise the rising time to suit yourself.

COTTAGE LOAVES

Cooking time 25–35 minutes
Oven temperature Hot
230°C, 450°F, Gas Mark 8
Makes 2 loaves

METRIC/IMPERIAL

900 g/2 lb plain flour	2 standard eggs
2 teaspoons sugar	6 tablespoons cooking oil
4 teaspoons dried yeast	2 teaspoons salt
450 ml/¾ pint milk, lukewarm	

Sift 275 g/10 oz of the flour into a mixing bowl. Add sugar, yeast and lukewarm (NOT hot) milk. Mix well, then leave in a warm place for about 20 minutes until frothy. Add beaten eggs, oil, remaining sifted flour and salt. Beat well.

Turn dough on to a lightly floured board and knead and stretch well for 10 minutes until the dough is elastic and no longer sticky. Shape the dough into a neat round and place in an oiled polythene bag. Loosely tie the bag and place in a bowl. Allow to rise in a warm place for 45–60 minutes, longer in a cool one, until the dough is double its size and springs back when pressed with a finger.

Turn dough on to a board, flatten firmly to knock out any air bubbles. Knead lightly, then divide into two. Cut off a third of the dough from each. Shape the larger piece into a neat round and place on a greased baking tray. Shape the remaining piece into a slightly smaller round and place on top.

Press the handle of a wooden spoon right through the centre of the loaves. Cover with a damp cloth, then leave to prove in a warm place for 20–30 minutes. Dust loaves with flour and bake on centre shelf of a hot oven for approximately 25–35 minutes until golden brown and crusty. When cooked, the loaves should sound hollow if tapped on the base. Place on a wire rack and cool.

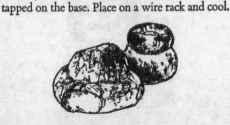

QUICK WHEATMEAL BREAD

Cooking time   30–40 minutes
Oven temperature   Hot
230°C, 450°F, Gas Mark 8
Makes 1 450-g/1-lb loaf and 3 50-g/2-oz rolls

METRIC/IMPERIAL

15 g/½ oz fresh yeast or
  2 teaspoons dried yeast
450 g/1 lb mixed plain flours,
  wholemeal and white in any
  proportion you like

2 teaspoons each salt and sugar
300 ml/½ pint water

Using fresh yeast

Rub yeast into flour, salt and sugar, add all the water and mix to a
soft dough, using your hand or a wooden spoon. Work to a smooth
dough, adding more flour if needed, until the dough leaves sides of
the basin clean.

Using dried yeast

Add a teaspoon of sugar to a cup of the water used in recipe (to get
best results the water should be warmed to 45°C/110°F, or hand-
hot). Sprinkle the dried yeast on top. Leave until frothy – about 10
minutes. Add to the flour, salt and remaining sugar with rest of liquid,
dough up and knead thoroughly on a floured board.

To make loaves

To make 1 450-g/1-lb loaf and 3 50-g/2-oz rolls: half fill well-
greased 450-g/1-lb loaf pan with dough. Put inside a large greased
polythene bag, loosely tied, and allow to rise to double size, 45–60
minutes in a warm place, longer in a cool one. Remove bag. Bake
on middle shelf of a hot oven for 30–40 minutes. Turn out on a wire
rack and cool.

HARVEST LOAF

Cooking time   30–40 minutes
Oven temperature   Hot
230°C, 450°F, Gas Mark 8
Makes 1 loaf 23 cm/9 inches long

METRIC/IMPERIAL

15 g/½ oz fresh yeast or	15 g/½ oz lard
2 teaspoons dried yeast	*for egg wash*
250 ml/scant ½ pint warm water	1 egg
450 g/1 lb plain flour	pinch sugar
2 teaspoons salt	

For yeast liquid

Blend 15 g/½ oz fresh yeast in 250 ml/½ pint less 2 tablespoons warm water OR dissolve 1 teaspoon sugar in 250 ml/½ pint less 2 tablespoons warm water, sprinkle on 2 teaspoons dried yeast and leave until frothy – about 10 minutes.

To make loaf

Mix the flour and salt in a bowl, rub in lard. Add the yeast liquid all at once and mix to a firm dough, adding extra flour if needed until dough leaves the sides of the bowl clean. Turn on to a lightly floured board and knead until dough is smooth (about 10 minutes). Leave to rise in a bowl covered with a lid or lightly greased polythene bag until dough is double in size, about 45–60 minutes in a warm place, longer in a cool one.

Punch dough well to knock out any large air bubbles. Divide into four pieces. Roll three of the pieces into 50-cm/20-inch long strands and join together at one end. Place on a lightly greased baking tray and plait loosely together; tuck ends underneath. Brush with egg wash. Divide fourth piece into two and roll each to a 50-cm/20-inch long strand. Join together at one end and twist strands loosely. Lay twist along centre of plait and tuck ends underneath.

Brush twist with egg wash. Leave to rise at room temperature, covered with greased polythene, until dough springs back when pressed lightly, about 30 minutes. Bake in a hot oven for 30–40 minutes.

For egg wash

Beat the egg and pinch of sugar with a little water.

DATE LOAF

Cooking time 1¼–1½ hours
Oven temperature Cool
150°C, 300°F, Gas Mark 2
Makes 1 loaf

METRIC/IMPERIAL

225 g/8 oz plain flour
1 teaspoon bicarbonate of soda
225 g/8 oz stoned dates

150 ml/¼ pint water
75 g/3 oz butter or margarine
1 egg

Grease and line a 1-kg/2-lb loaf pan with greased greaseproof paper. Sift the flour with the bicarbonate of soda. Finely chop the dates and place in a small saucepan with the water. Heat together until soft. Remove from heat and beat well with a wooden spoon until smooth. Mix in the butter or margarine and allow to cool for 5 minutes.

Stir in the beaten egg then beat in flour mixture. Pour into prepared pan and bake in a cool oven for 1¼–1½ hours or until spongy to touch. Turn on to a wire tray, remove paper and leave to cool. Store two days in an airtight tin before cutting. Serve in slices spread with butter.

GLAZED CHERRY BREAD

Cooking time 1 hour 5 minutes
Oven temperature Moderate
160°C, 325°F, Gas Mark 3
Makes 2 loaves

METRIC/IMPERIAL

350 g/12 oz self-raising
flour
1 teaspoon salt
50 g/2 oz castor sugar
50 g/2 oz walnuts, chopped
50 g/2 oz dates, stoned and
chopped
2 tablespoons malt extract

50 g/2 oz butter or margarine
150 ml/¼ pint milk
2 eggs
for glaze and topping
50 g/2 oz castor sugar
2 tablespoons water
25 g/1 oz walnuts
40 g/1½ oz glacé cherries

Well grease two 450-g/1-lb loaf tins. Sift the flour and salt into a bowl, add sugar, walnuts and dates. Gently heat malt and butter or margarine until the fat has melted. Pour into the centre of the flour mixture with the blended milk and eggs. Mix together to a smooth, soft dough. Turn into the two prepared loaf tins. Bake for 1 hour in a moderate oven.

For glaze and topping

Heat sugar and water in a pan and boil for 2–3 minutes until syrupy. When the loaves are cooked, turn out on to a wire rack and brush tops at once with glaze; decorate with nuts and cherries.

NUTTY ORANGE BREAD

Cooking time   1 hour
Oven temperature   Moderate
180°C, 350°F, Gas Mark 4
Makes 1 loaf

METRIC/IMPERIAL

350 g/12 oz self-raising flour	2 medium eggs, well beaten
½ teaspoon salt	about 150 ml/¼ pint cold milk
75 g/3 oz castor sugar	50 g/2 oz butter or margarine,
40 g/1½ oz walnuts, coarsely	melted
chopped	*for glaze*
50 g/2 oz candied orange peel,	1 tablespoon castor sugar
finely chopped	1 tablespoon milk

Grease a 1-kg/2-lb loaf tin. Sift the flour and salt into a bowl then stir in sugar, walnuts and peel. Mix to a slack consistency with the eggs and milk, stirring well. Fold in the melted fat, then turn mixture into the prepared tin. Bake in the centre of a moderate oven for 1 hour. Turn out on to a wire tray and brush top immediately with glaze.

Cut into slices when cold and serve with whipped cream and chunky strawberry jam.

For glaze

Put sugar and milk into a pan, heat until sugar dissolves then boil briskly for 3 minutes or until syrupy.

WHOLEWHEAT SCONES

Cooking time   10–15 minutes
Oven temperature   Hot
220°C, 425°F, Gas Mark 7
Makes 12 scones

METRIC/IMPERIAL

110 g/4 oz plain flour
1 teaspoon baking powder
1 teaspoon salt
110 g/4 oz wholewheat flour

50 g/2 oz butter, margarine or
    cooking fat
2 teaspoons sugar
about 150 ml/¼ pint milk
milk to glaze

Lightly flour a baking tray. Sift plain flour, baking powder and salt together. Stir in wholewheat flour. Rub in fat finely. Stir in sugar, mix to a soft dough with milk. Knead lightly, then roll out on a floured board and cut into rounds with a plain pastry cutter. Place on prepared baking tray, brush tops with milk. Bake near the top of a hot oven for 10–15 minutes until risen. Cool on a wire rack.

BUTTERSCOTCH SCONES

Cooking time   15–20 minutes
Oven temperature   Hot
230°C, 450°F, Gas Mark 8
Makes 8 scones

METRIC/IMPERIAL

350 g/12 oz self-raising flour
50 g/2 oz butter
25 g/1 oz castor sugar
grated rind of 1 orange
1 egg
about 6 tablespoons milk

2 heaped tablespoons orange
    marmalade
50 g/2 oz currants
for topping
25 g/1 oz melted butter
25 g/1 oz brown sugar

Sift the flour, rub in the butter and stir in the castor sugar and orange rind. Add the beaten egg and milk, mixing to a soft but not sticky dough. Turn out on to a floured board, knead lightly to a smooth ball; roll to a rectangle about 30 by 23 cm/12 by 9 inches. Spread with marmalade, not quite to the edge, and sprinkle with currants. Roll up like a Swiss roll. Cut into thick slices.

For topping

Pour the melted butter into a shallow square or round cake pan, about 20 cm/8 inches across. Butter sides and sprinkle bottom with brown sugar. Arrange scones in the pan, not quite touching each other. Bake in a hot oven for 15–20 minutes.

HUNTER'S ROLLS

Cooking time   15 minutes
Oven temperature   Hot
220°C, 425°F, Gas Mark 7
Makes 6 rolls

METRIC/IMPERIAL

175 g/6 oz short crust or flaky pastry (see page 69)
for filling
100 g/4 oz corned beef
1 apple, peeled, cored and chopped

2 teaspoons chopped pickled walnuts
2 teaspoons horseradish cream
beaten egg
salt and pepper

Roll out pastry on a lightly floured board and cut into six pieces, 10 by 8 cm/4 by 3 inches. Finely chop the corned beef. Mix with apple, pickled walnuts and horseradish cream, bind with a little beaten egg. Season to taste. Roll the filling into six sausage shapes and place one on each piece of pastry, damp round pastry edges and roll up, press edges firmly together to seal. Place on a baking tray and brush tops with beaten egg. Bake in a hot oven for about 15 minutes. Serve hot or cold.

MARMALADE RING

Cooking time   45 minutes
Oven temperature   Moderate
180°C, 350°F, Gas Mark 4
Makes 1 ring

METRIC/IMPERIAL

350g/12oz self-raising flour
75 g/3 oz butter
75 g/3 oz soft brown sugar
50 g/2 oz sultanas
1 medium egg
scant 150 ml/¼ pint milk

3 tablespoons coarsely cut
orange marmalade
for icing
2 tablespoons marmalade
50 g/2 oz sieved icing sugar

Sift the flour into a mixing bowl. Rub in butter until mixture resembles fine breadcrumbs. Stir in sugar and sultanas. Add the lightly beaten egg, milk and marmalade. Mix to a smooth dough. Shape dough into a 30-cm/12-inch roll, then form into a ring.

Place ring on a greased baking tray and bake in a moderate oven for 45 minutes. Allow to cool.

For icing

Gently heat the marmalade until hot, then stir in icing sugar. Pour icing over the baked ring.

GINGER NUTS

Cooking time   15–20 minutes
Oven temperature   Moderate
180°C, 350°F, Gas Mark 4
Makes 12 ginger nuts

METRIC/IMPERIAL

225 g/8 oz plain flour
1 teaspoon bicarbonate of soda
1 teaspoon ground ginger
50 g/2 oz lard

50 g/2 oz margarine
75 g/3 oz soft brown sugar
1 tablespoon golden syrup
1 tablespoon lemon juice

Grease two baking trays. Sift the flour, soda and ginger together. Melt the fats in a saucepan (do not allow to boil), add the sugar, golden syrup and lemon juice and pour into the flour, mixing very thoroughly. Roll into balls about the size of a small walnut.

Place on prepared baking tray, allowing a little room for spreading during cooking. Flatten each slightly with a damped finger. Bake in a moderate oven for 15–20 minutes. Leave to firm on the baking tray for a few minutes before lifting on to a rack to cool.

FLAPJACKS

Cooking time   30 minutes
Oven temperature   Moderate
160°C, 325°F, Gas Mark 3
Makes 12 flapjacks

METRIC/IMPERIAL

50 g/2 oz margarine	50 g/2 oz golden syrup
50 g/2 oz sugar	100 g/4 oz rolled oats
50 g/2 oz black treacle	

Melt the margarine in a pan with sugar, black treacle and golden syrup. When melted gently stir in the oats. Press into a Swiss roll tin.

Bake in a moderate oven for 30 minutes. Mark into triangles while hot, leave in the tin until cold, then remove separately.

CHOCOLATE BROWNIES

Cooking time   30 minutes
Oven temperature   Moderately hot
190°C, 375°F, Gas Mark 5
Makes 18 brownies

METRIC/IMPERIAL

110 g/4 oz butter or margarine	$\frac{1}{2}$ teaspoon baking powder
225 g/8 oz soft brown sugar	good pinch salt
2 eggs	*for topping*
110 g/4 oz plain flour	castor sugar
40 g/1½ oz cocoa powder	

Grease a Swiss roll tin. Cream the butter and sugar together until light and fluffy. Add eggs, one at a time, beating thoroughly after each addition. Sift together the flour, cocoa powder, baking powder and salt. Stir into creamed mixture until well blended. Spread mixture in prepared tin.

Bake in a moderately hot oven for about 30 minutes, until firm to the touch in centre. Sprinkle with castor sugar while hot and cut in squares while still warm.

WALNUT AND DATE COOKIES

Cooking time   10–12 minutes
Oven temperature   Moderately hot
200°C, 400°F, Gas Mark 6
Makes about 16 cookies

METRIC/IMPERIAL

75 g/3 oz self-raising flour
25 g/1 oz fine semolina
50 g/2 oz butter or margarine
40 g/1½ oz castor sugar

50 g/2 oz dates, chopped
25 g/1 oz walnuts, finely chopped
1 medium egg

Well grease a baking tray. Sift the flour into a mixing bowl, add semolina and rub in the fat lightly. Add sugar and the finely chopped dates and walnuts. Mix to a stiff consistency with the well-beaten egg. Pile large teaspoons of the mixture on the prepared baking tray.

Bake towards the top in a moderately hot oven for 10–12 minutes. Cool on a wire tray.

MELTING MOMENTS

Cooking time   15–20 minutes
Oven temperature   Moderate
180°C, 350°F, Gas Mark 4
Makes 20 cakes

METRIC/IMPERIAL

100 g/4 oz margarine

75 g/3 oz castor sugar

½ beaten egg

150 g/5 oz self-raising flour

scant ½ teaspoon vanilla essence

25 g/1 oz rolled oats

Grease a baking tray. Cream the margarine with sugar until soft and fluffy. Stir in beaten egg. Fold in sifted flour. Add vanilla essence. Spread rolled oats on a board or greaseproof paper. Use a teaspoon to form the mixture into small balls and dip the tops in oats to coat. Arrange on prepared baking tray, allow spreading room.

Bake in a moderate oven for 15–20 minutes or until golden brown. Leave a half minute on tray, lift on to wire rack to cool.

HONEY SANDWICH

Cooking time 25–30 minutes
Oven temperature   Moderate
180°C, 350°F, Gas Mark 4
Makes 1 cake

METRIC/IMPERIAL

for sandwich cake

175 g/6 oz butter or margarine

110 g/4 oz castor sugar

1 tablespoon clear honey

3 eggs

175 g/6 oz self-raising flour

pinch salt

2 tablespoons hot water

sugar for dredging

for honey butter filling

110 g/4 oz butter

175 g/6 oz icing sugar

2 tablespoons clear honey

Grease and line the base of two 18–20-cm/7–8-inch sandwich cake tins with greased greaseproof paper. Cream the butter or margarine with the sugar and honey until really light and fluffy. Lightly whisk eggs and gradually beat into the creamed mixture. Carefully fold in sifted flour, salt and a little water. Divide mixture between prepared tins, smooth over tops with palette knife. Bake just above the centre of a moderate oven for about 25–30 minutes or until golden brown and springy to the touch. Turn on to a wire rack to cool and strip off the paper. When quite cold sandwich together with the prepared honey butter filling and dredge the top well with castor sugar.

For honey butter filling

Cream the butter until very light and fluffy. Gradually beat in the sifted icing sugar until smooth and creamy, then stir in the honey until well blended.

GOLDEN HONEY CAKE

Cooking time   about 1 hour
Oven temperature   Moderate
180°C, 350°F, Gas Mark 4
Makes 1 cake

METRIC/IMPERIAL

110 g/4 oz butter or margarine	225 g/8 oz self-raising flour,
110 g/4 oz castor sugar	sifted
3 eggs	pinch salt
110 g/4 oz (2 tablespoons) clear	milk to moisten
honey	

Line a greased 18-cm/7-inch round cake tin with greased greaseproof paper. Cream the butter or margarine with castor sugar until light and fluffy. Gradually beat in the whisked eggs and the honey with a little of the sifted flour and a pinch of salt. Fold in the remaining sifted flour with sufficient milk to make a soft dropping consistency.

Turn into prepared tin and bake in the centre of a moderate oven for about 1 hour, or until golden and cooked through. Cool and serve cut into slices. Spread with butter if desired.

CHERRY CAKE

Cooking time   1¼ hours
Oven temperature   Moderate
180°C, 350°F, Gas Mark 4
Makes 1 cake

METRIC/IMPERIAL

110 g/4 oz butter
110 g/4 oz castor sugar
2 medium eggs
3 tablespoons milk
1 teaspoon grated lemon rind
¼ teaspoon vanilla essence
175 g/6 oz plain flour

pinch salt
1 teaspoon baking powder
25 g/1 oz ground almonds
25 g/1 oz semolina
75 g/3 oz glacé cherries, halved
    and quartered

Line a greased 15-cm/6-inch round cake tin with greased greaseproof paper. Cream the butter and sugar very well together, add the eggs gradually, beating between each addition. Scrape down the sides of the bowl, add the milk, lemon rind and vanilla essence and beat again to ensure even mixing.

Sift the flour, salt and baking powder together, then with a metal spoon fold into the creamed mixture together with the almonds, semolina and cherries. Scrape down the sides of the bowl and fold again lightly. Put into prepared tin and bake on the middle shelf of a moderate oven for about 1¼ hours.

VICTORIA SANDWICH

Cooking time   25–30 minutes
Oven temperature   Moderate
180°C, 350°F, Gas Mark 4
Makes 1 cake

METRIC/IMPERIAL

110 g/4 oz self-raising flour
pinch salt
110 g/4 oz butter or margarine,
    or mixture of both
110 g/4 oz castor sugar

2 medium eggs
about 2 tablespoons raspberry jam
2–3 teaspoons castor sugar for
    top

Grease two 15–18-cm/6–7-inch sandwich cake tins. Sift flour and salt. Cream fat and sugar until light and fluffy, then beat in eggs, one at a time. Fold in flour with a metal spoon, then divide mixture equally between prepared tins, smoothing top of mixture. Bake in the centre of moderate oven for 25–30 minutes. Turn out and cool on a wire tray. When cold fill with jam and dust with castor sugar.

RICH FRUIT CAKE

Cooking time   2½–3 hours
Oven temperature   Cool
150°C, 300°F, Gas Mark 2
Makes 1 cake

METRIC/IMPERIAL

250 g/9 oz plain flour
1 teaspoon baking powder
pinch salt
225 g/8 oz butter or margarine
225 g/8 oz castor sugar
3 eggs
finely grated rind of 1 orange

100 g/4 oz each: cleaned currants, sultanas, seedless raisins
50 g/2 oz chopped peel
50 g/2 oz ground almonds
50 g/2 oz glacé cherries, cut
1 tablespoon sherry or milk

Grease and line a 20-cm/8-inch cake tin with greased greaseproof paper. Sift the flour with baking powder and salt. Cream the butter or margarine with the sugar until light and fluffy. Gradually beat in one egg at a time with 1 tablespoon of the sifted ingredients. Stir in the grated orange rind, the currants, sultanas, raisins, peel, almonds and cherries. Fold in the remaining flour mixture, then stir in the sherry or milk.

Turn into prepared tin and smooth over the top with a palette knife. Bake in the centre of a cool oven for 2½–3 hours or until golden brown and firm to touch. Cool for 30 minutes in tin, then turn out and cool on a wire rack, remove paper. Store in an airtight tin.

SPICED RAISIN CAKE

Cooking time   1¼ hours
Oven temperature   Moderate
180°C, 350°F, Gas Mark 4
Makes 1 cake

METRIC/IMPERIAL

225 g/8 oz butter	*for filling and topping*
175 g/6 oz soft brown sugar	50 g/2 oz walnuts, chopped
2 tablespoons treacle	25 g/1 oz soft brown sugar
2 eggs	1 teaspoon powdered cinnamon
275 g/10 oz self-raising flour	50 g/2 oz seedless raisins, chopped
6 tablespoons milk	

Mix the filling and topping ingredients together. Well grease an
18 by 28-cm/7 by 11-inch ovenproof dish. Cream butter and sugar
until light and fluffy. Blend treacle with eggs and gradually beat into
creamed mixture. Fold in the flour and milk. Put half of mixture into
prepared dish, cover with half of fruit and nut mixture. Add rest of
the cake mixture and top with remaining fruit and nut mixture.

Bake in a moderate oven for about 1 hour 15 minutes. Cut into
squares and serve hot.

OLD-ENGLISH CIDER CAKE

Cooking time   45–50 minutes
Oven temperature   Moderate
160°C, 325°F, Gas Mark 3
Makes 1 cake

METRIC/IMPERIAL

225 g/8 oz plain flour	110 g/4 oz butter or margarine
pinch nutmeg	110 g/4 oz castor sugar
½ teaspoon ground ginger	2 eggs
½ teaspoon bicarbonate of soda	150 ml/¼ pint cider

Grease a shallow baking pan about 20 by 15 cm/8 by 6 inches, with
sloping sides. Sift the dry ingredients. Cream the butter and sugar
until light. Beat in the eggs, one at a time. Stir in half the flour. Whisk
the cider until frothy, then stir into mixture. Fold in remaining flour.
Place mixture in the prepared pan. Bang the pan gently to settle
mixture.

Bake in centre of a moderate oven for 45–50 minutes. Leave one day before cutting.

CUT AND COME AGAIN CAKE

Cooking time   about 1½ hours
Oven temperature   Moderate
180°C, 350°F, Gas Mark 4
Makes 1 cake

METRIC/IMPERIAL

450 g/1 lb plain flour	100 g/4 oz currants
1 teaspoon salt	100 g/4 oz glacé cherries,
2 teaspoons baking powder	chopped
2 teaspoons mixed spice	2 eggs
175 g/6 oz butter or margarine	25 g/1 oz warmed golden syrup
175 g/6 oz castor sugar	300 ml/½ pint milk
100 g/4 oz raisins	

Line a 20-cm/8-inch round cake tin with greased greaseproof paper. Sift the flour, salt, baking powder and mixed spice together into a large bowl. Rub in fat lightly until mixture resembles fine breadcrumbs. Stir in sugar, cleaned raisins, currants and cherries.

Whisk together the eggs, golden syrup and most of the milk. Add to dry ingredients and mix to a soft consistency, beating well, adding remaining milk if necessary. Turn into prepared tin. Bake on shelf below centre in a moderate oven for approximately 1½ hours, or until well risen and cooked through. Cool, remove paper and store in an airtight tin.

STICKY GINGERBREAD

Cooking time 40–50 minutes
Oven temperature Moderate
180°C, 350°F, Gas Mark 4
Makes 1 cake

METRIC/IMPERIAL

350 g/12 oz plain flour	175 g/6 oz butter or margarine
pinch salt	3 tablespoons golden syrup
1½ teaspoons mixed spice	3 tablespoons black treacle
4½ teaspoons ground ginger	1½ teaspoons bicarbonate of soda
65 g/2½ oz demerara sugar	200 ml/7 fl oz warm milk
65 g/2½ oz sultanas	1 beaten egg

Grease and line an 18-cm/7-inch square pan with greased greaseproof paper. Sift the flour, salt and spices into a mixing bowl. Stir in demerara sugar and sultanas. Place fat together with the syrup and treacle in a saucepan. Stir over a gentle heat until melted. Add to the dry ingredients and beat well. Dissolve bicarbonate of soda in the warm milk and add beaten egg. Pour this into the prepared mixture and beat well to form a smooth batter. Pour into the prepared pan.

Bake on centre shelf of a moderate oven for 40–50 minutes until well risen and springy to the touch. Cool slightly in the pan, then turn on to a wire rack; remove paper.

Note Store in airtight tin for 2–3 days before use.

The Country Hostess

Entertaining is an important part of country life and the aim of most country hostesses is to provide a well-spread table. This is especially true at times of festivity, such as Christmas. But the problems of dinner-party giving are the same in town or country. Here are a few tips to help you be a successful hostess:

Never try out a new dish for the first time on 'the night' – practise it first.

Write out a timetable to act as a working guide.

Have a definite colour scheme for the table setting; blend china, napkins, flowers and candles. Set the table in the morning.

For lavish effect serve food on large platters for guests to help themselves.

Follow recipes carefully – don't take short cuts, they may land you in trouble.

Cover dishes of hot food tightly with kitchen foil and put in a warm place to keep hot.

To keep gravy or sauce hot without it sticking to the saucepan, stand it in a meat pan half-filled with simmering water in the oven. Cover the top of the sauce with wetted greaseproof paper to prevent a skin forming.

Make sure you've got ready to hand kitchen foil, a bottle opener, a really sharp kitchen knife, plenty of dried herbs and simple things like salt, pepper and mustard.

Meal Starters

MUSHROOM SOUP

Cooking time   about 1 hour
Serves 4

METRIC/IMPERIAL

225 g/8 oz mushrooms	25 g/1 oz flour
1 onion, chopped	450 ml/¾ pint milk
25 g/1 oz butter	salt and pepper
600 ml/1 pint stock	4 tablespoons single cream

Wipe and finely slice the mushrooms, chop the onion. Melt the butter in a saucepan and sauté the mushrooms and onion for 2–3 minutes until soft. Add the stock. Blend the flour with a little of the milk and add gradually to the soup with the rest of the milk.

Season to taste. Bring to the boil stirring all the while and simmer for 45 minutes to 1 hour. Add the cream before serving but do not allow to boil.

CELERY AND HERB SOUP

Cooking time 1 hour 10 minutes
Serves 4

METRIC/IMPERIAL

1 head celery, washed and chopped	pinch thyme
1 onion, sliced	1 bay leaf
1 carrot, sliced	1 teaspoon chopped parsley
25 g/1 oz butter	salt and pepper
450 ml/¾ pint stock	25 g/1 oz flour
	450 ml/¾ pint milk

Sauté prepared vegetables very gently in the melted butter in a pan for 5 minutes. Add stock, herbs and seasoning. Bring to the boil and simmer for 1 hour until vegetables are soft. Sieve the soup or put in a liquidiser. Blend the flour with a little milk, add with the rest of the milk to the soup. Bring to the boil and cook for 2–3 minutes. Garnish with chopped fresh herbs, if liked.

PEAR APPETISERS

Serves 4

METRIC/IMPERIAL

4 ripe pears	salt and pepper
lemon juice	4 teaspoons chopped parsley
100 g/4 oz cream cheese	100 g/4 oz ham, sliced and chopped
4 teaspoons mayonnaise or salad cream	lettuce
4 tablespoons thick cream	

Peel the pears, slice in half and remove cores. Dip the pear halves in lemon juice to preserve colour. Mix together the cream cheese, mayonnaise, cream and seasoning. Fold the chopped parsley and ham into the mixture. Pile mixture on to pear halves, and arrange two pear halves per person on lettuce on individual dishes.

GRAPEFRUIT CUPS

Serves 4

METRIC/IMPERIAL

2 grapefruit

50 g/2 oz castor sugar

2 oranges

2 dessert apples, cored and sliced

4 maraschino cherries

Halve the grapefruit, remove segments and chop the fruit, flute edges
of the grapefruit cups. Arrange the fruit in the base of the grapefruit
cups and dredge with castor sugar. Peel the oranges and divide into
segments. Arrange orange segments and apple slices on chopped
grapefruit. Dredge with castor sugar. Decorate with cherries and
serve chilled.

SUMMER PÂTÉ

Cooking time   10 minutes
Serves 4

METRIC/IMPERIAL

100 g/4 oz soft herring roes

salt and pepper

75 g/3 oz butter

2 teaspoons lemon juice

2 teaspoons chopped parsley

Season the roes with salt and pepper and gently fry in a little butter
for 10 minutes. Pound to a fine paste with a wooden spoon. Soften
the rest of the butter, add to roe paste. Add lemon juice and parsley.
Serve with Melba toast or brown bread and butter.

BACON TOASTS

Cooking time   10 minutes
Serves 4

METRIC/IMPERIAL

4 slices bread

butter

4 tomatoes, sliced

4 slices Cheddar cheese

4 rashers bacon, rinds removed

Toast the bread slices lightly on both sides. Remove crusts. Spread
lightly with butter. Cover with a layer of tomato, and top with a

slice of cheese. Cut bacon rashers in half and arrange on top of cheese. Grill until the cheese melts and turns golden, and the bacon is crisp.

Main Course Specials

PINEAPPLE GAMMON STEAKS

Cooking time about 20 minutes
Serves 2

METRIC/IMPERIAL

2 gammon steaks	3 tablespoons golden syrup or
1 (425-g/15-oz) can pineapple	brown sugar
rings	watercress

Snip edges of the gammon steaks with scissors. Strain the juice from pineapple into a pan. Add gammon steaks. Cover with a plate, carrying the pineapple rings. Cover with foil or lid. Poach gently until tender, about 15 minutes.

Put steaks on a flameproof dish surrounded with pineapple. Cover all lightly with golden syrup or brown sugar. Place under hot grill for about 2 minutes. Serve pineapple on steaks topped with watercress. Pour a little of the liquor round each.

SAVOURY BACON PIE

Cooking time 1¾ hours
Oven temperature Moderately hot
190°C, 375°F, Gas Mark 5
Serves 4

METRIC/IMPERIAL

2 sheep's kidneys	100 g/4 oz cheese, grated
100 g/4 oz mushrooms	salt and pepper
25 g/1 oz butter	300 ml/½ pint stock made with
6 rashers middle cut bacon	meat cube
675 g/1½ lb potatoes, peeled and	
sliced	

Skin, core and quarter the kidneys. Quarter the mushrooms. Fry together 2 minutes in butter. Remove rind from bacon and cut two rashers into pieces. In a shallow casserole, place first a layer of sliced potato, then cheese, kidneys, mushrooms and chopped bacon, finishing with potatoes.

Arrange four rashers of bacon lengthwise, across top of casserole. Season stock, pour into casserole. Cover with lid or foil. Bake in the centre of a moderately hot oven for 1 hour. Remove lid. Continue baking for 30 to 45 minutes, until brown.

HONEY-BAKED BACON

Cooking time   about 1 hour
Oven temperature   Moderately hot
190°C, 375°F, Gas Mark 5
Serves 4

METRIC/IMPERIAL

575 g/1¼ lb middle or corner gammon	1 small onion, skinned
1 bay leaf	2 tablespoons clear honey
pepper	½ teacup hot water

Leave the bacon to soak in cold water for 4 hours (or overnight). If packeted then follow instructions on label. Drain. Put into pan and cover with fresh water. Add the bay leaf, pepper and onion. Bring to the boil then simmer for 20 minutes per half kilo/per lb or until tender. Drain and remove rind while joint is hot.

Put bacon in a meat pan. Mix honey with the hot water and pour over bacon. Cook for 30 minutes in moderately hot oven, basting twice during cooking.

BEEF TERRINE

Cooking time   1¼–1½ hours
Oven temperature   Moderate
180°C, 350°F, Gas Mark 4
Makes 10 slices

METRIC/IMPERIAL

675 g/1½ lb minced beef

100 g/4 oz pork sausage meat

2 teaspoons made mustard

salt and pepper

2 good pinches dried tarragon
  (optional)

1 medium onion, chopped

1 egg, beaten

1 clove garlic, crushed

15 g/½ oz butter

15 g/½ oz plain flour

150 ml/¼ pint milk

to garnish

tomato wedges

chopped parsley

In a large bowl mix the minced beef, sausage meat, mustard, seasonings, tarragon, onion, egg and garlic. Make a thin white sauce in the usual way with the butter, flour and milk and blend into the meat mixture. Mix well until smooth. Grease a pâté or loaf tin and press the mixture in, smoothing the top. Cover with aluminium foil and cook in a moderate oven. Leave to cool. Turn out into a dish and remove any excess fat round the edges. Garnish with tomato wedges and chopped parsley. Serve sliced with mixed salad.

JUGGED HARE WITH FORCEMEAT BALLS

Cooking time   about 3 hours 10 minutes
Oven temperature   Moderate
160°C, 325°F, Gas Mark 3
Serves 4–6

METRIC/IMPERIAL

1 hare

25–50 g/1–2 oz dripping

1 rasher bacon

900 ml/1½ pints stock or water

40 g/1½ oz flour, blended with a
   little stock

1 onion stuck with 2 cloves

salt and pepper

bouquet garni

1 small bay leaf

4 peppercorns

small blade mace

2 teaspoons redcurrant jelly

150 ml/¼ pint port or other type
   of red wine

for forcemeat balls

100 g/4 oz fresh white
   breadcrumbs

50 g/2 oz shredded suet

2 teaspoons chopped parsley

a little grated lemon rind

1 teaspoon chopped thyme

squeeze of lemon juice

salt and pepper

beaten egg to bind

1 tablespoon flour

fat for frying

Skin and paunch the hare, reserving the blood. Wipe the hare and cut into joints. Heat the dripping in a saucepan or flameproof casserole and fry joints in it with the chopped bacon. When the meat is lightly browned, add stock to cover, stir in the blended flour, the onion, seasoning and herbs, etc. Cover and cook very gently on top of cooker or in a moderate oven for about 3 hours, or until tender. A few minutes before serving, remove the onion and bunch of herbs. Stir in the strained blood, redcurrant jelly and wine. Reheat without boiling. Garnish with cooked forcemeat balls.

To make forcemeat balls

Mix together the breadcrumbs, suet, parsley, lemon rind, thyme, lemon juice and seasoning. Add sufficient beaten egg to bind. Form into small balls and toss in flour to coat. Fry in hot fat, turning until golden brown and cooked through, about 10 minutes.

ROAST TURKEY WITH CHESTNUT STUFFING AND ACCOMPANIMENTS

Cooking time   3 hours 20 minutes–4 hours
Oven temperature   Moderate
160°C, 325°F, Gas Mark 3;
hot 220°C, 425°F, Gas Mark 7 for last 30 minutes
Serves 8

METRIC/IMPERIAL

4–5 kg/10–12 lb dressed turkey
salt
100 g/4 oz butter, softened
50 g/2 oz fat bacon
225 g/8 oz streaky bacon
450 g/1 lb chipolata sausages
for chestnut stuffing
450 g/1 lb chestnuts
300 ml/½ pint milk and water
  mixed

100 g/4 oz white breadcrumbs
50 g/2 oz sausage meat
1 teaspoon mixed herbs
rind of 1 lemon, finely grated
salt and freshly ground black
  pepper
little beaten egg

Wipe the turkey inside and out with a clean damp cloth. Place the prepared stuffing in neck end of the turkey. Wrap flap of skin over it and secure with a small skewer. Weigh turkey and calculate the cooking time, allowing 20 minutes per half kilo/per lb. Place turkey in meat pan, rub salt over skin then spread with butter.

Trim rind from fat bacon, place rashers over breast of bird. Cover closely with kitchen foil. Cook in a moderate oven for required cooking period. Meanwhile, trim rind from streaky bacon, flatten rashers with palette knife, roll up into neat rolls. Thread sausages and bacon rolls on to skewers. Thirty minutes before the end of turkey cooking time, increase oven temperature to hot. Remove foil and fat bacon. Drain off most of the juices and fat, set aside for gravy. Place sausages and bacon rolls round turkey to cook. Replace in oven for 30 minutes. Transfer turkey to serving dish, arrange trimmings. Serve with gravy and bread sauce (see below).

For chestnut stuffing

Slit chestnuts on flat side and roast on a baking tray in a hot oven for 15 minutes. Peel off skins while warm as they are more difficult to peel when cool. Put nuts on to boil in milk and water, reduce heat and simmer for 15 minutes until tender. Strain off liquid, reserve. Finely chop nuts or mince through a coarse-bladed mincer. Add remaining ingredients to nuts. Bind together with cooking liquid and beaten egg if necessary.

ROAST GOOSE WITH SAGE AND ONION STUFFING

Cooking time   about 4–5 hours
Oven temperature   Moderately hot
200°C, 400°F, Gas Mark 6 for 15 minutes;
moderate 180°C, 350°F, Gas Mark 4 for rest of time
Serves 6–8

METRIC/IMPERIAL

4–5 kg/10–12 lb dressed goose	75 g/3 oz butter
4 lemons	4 teaspoons dried sage
salt and freshly ground black pepper	225 g/8 oz white breadcrumbs
parsley	salt and freshly ground black pepper
for sage and onion stuffing	1 egg
675 g/1½ lb onions	

Wipe the goose well inside and out with a clean damp cloth. Place prepared stuffing in neck end of goose, wrap flap over and secure with a small skewer. Weigh bird and calculate the cooking time, allowing 25 minutes per half kilo/per lb. Cut two lemons in half, place them inside goose. Place goose in meat pan, rub seasoning over skin. Pour over goose strained lemon juice from remaining lemons. Do not add any fat as goose is sufficiently fatty. Cook in a moderately hot oven for 15 minutes. Reduce heat to moderate and cook for remaining time until tender. Carefully transfer goose to serving dish, garnish with parsley.

For sage and onion stuffing

Peel and finely chop onions. Cook in 50 g/2 oz melted butter for 5 minutes. Place in a bowl, add sage, breadcrumbs and seasoning. Bind together with remaining melted butter and lightly beaten egg.

GRAVY

Cooking time 5 minutes

METRIC/IMPERIAL

3–4 tablespoons dripping, and
sediment from turkey fat
2 tablespoons flour

600 ml/1 pint turkey stock, made
from giblets
gravy browning
salt and pepper

Heat the dripping from turkey fat in a saucepan. Stir in the flour and
gradually add stock made up to 600 ml/1 pint with water if necessary.
Bring to the boil and cook for 3–4 minutes. Add a few drops of
browning to make a rich colour. Season to taste.

BREAD SAUCE

Cooking time 10 minutes

METRIC/IMPERIAL

450 ml/¾ pint milk
1 onion, peeled
3 cloves
1 bay leaf

75 g/3 oz fresh white
breadcrumbs
25 g/1 oz butter
seasoning

Pour the milk into a saucepan and add the onion studded with cloves.
Add the bay leaf. Heat gently to simmering point. Remove from
heat and allow to stand for 1–2 hours. Strain the milk and return to
pan. Add breadcrumbs, together with butter. Season to taste and heat
slowly until the sauce is thick and creamy.

ROAST PHEASANT WITH MUSHROOMS

Cooking time   about 1 hour 10 minutes
Oven temperature   Hot
220°C, 425°F, Gas Mark 7 for 10 minutes;
then moderately hot 200°C, 400°F, Gas Mark 6
Serves 4

METRIC/IMPERIAL

2 pheasants, about 1.25 kg/2½ lb, dressed	salt and freshly ground black pepper
225 g/8 oz button mushrooms	4–6 rashers fat bacon
175 g/6 oz unsalted butter	

Wipe the pheasants inside and out with a clean damp cloth. Wipe mushrooms. Place about 1 tablespoon of mushrooms and 50 g/2 oz butter, in pats, inside each bird. Place pheasants in a meat pan, sprinkle with salt and freshly ground black pepper. Trim rind from bacon rashers, arrange over breasts of birds. Cover with a thickly buttered piece of greaseproof paper.

Cook pheasants on the centre shelf of a hot oven for 10 minutes, then reduce oven to moderately hot and continue cooking for about 1 hour or until pheasants are cooked. Ten minutes before the end of cooking time, remove paper and bacon, and baste pheasants well with juices from pan. Return to the oven to brown.

Simmer rest of the mushrooms in remaining melted butter for 5 minutes until tender; season to taste. Transfer cooked pheasants to hot serving dish. Drain the cooked mushrooms, spoon round the pheasants.

Festive Desserts

SYLLABUB

Serves 6–8

METRIC/IMPERIAL

juice and grated zest of 1 large lemon	50 g/2 oz castor sugar
	300 ml/½ pint double cream
4 tablespoons sweet sherry	4 ratafia biscuits
2 tablespoons brandy	

Put the lemon juice and grated zest, sherry, brandy and sugar in a bowl. Stir until the sugar has dissolved. Add the cream and whisk until mixture forms soft peaks. Spoon into individual glasses and serve chilled. Sprinkle with crushed ratafia biscuits.

CHRISTMAS PUDDING

Cooking time   6–8 hours, re-steaming 2–3 hours
Makes 2 puddings, 6–8 servings each

METRIC/IMPERIAL

450 g/1 lb seedless raisins	225 g/8 oz fresh white
225 g/8 oz currants	breadcrumbs
225 g/8 oz sultanas	¼ teaspoon grated nutmeg
100 g/4 oz chopped mixed peel	pinch salt
25 g/1 oz almonds, blanched	3 eggs, well beaten
and chopped	grated rind and juice of 1 lemon
175 g/6 oz self-raising flour	4–5 tablespoons rum
225 g/8 oz shredded suet	milk to mix
175 g/6 oz dark brown sugar	

Well grease two medium-sized pudding basins. Wash and dry fruits. Put all dry ingredients into a basin. Add eggs and lemon juice and mix well together. Add rum and enough milk to mix to a stiff dropping consistency. Mix very thoroughly, leave overnight if wished. Press mixture into prepared basins. Cover with two thicknesses greased greaseproof paper and pudding cloth, tie securely. Steam for 6–8 hours for each pudding.

Re-cover, re-steam for 2–3 hours before serving. Serve with brandy butter (see below).

BRANDY BUTTER

METRIC/IMPERIAL

100 g/4 oz unsalted butter	3–4 tablespoons brandy
100 g/4 oz castor sugar	

Cream the butter and sugar until light and fluffy, then gradually beat in the brandy. Pile into a serving dish. Leave in a cool place to set.

SHERRY CREAM TRIFLE

Serves 6

METRIC/IMPERIAL

8 small sponge cakes
2–3 tablespoons raspberry jam
3 tablespoons sherry
50 g/2 oz crushed ratafia biscuits
600 ml/1 pint hot custard
300 ml/½ pint double cream

25 g/1 oz castor sugar
for decoration
split blanched almonds
halved glacé cherries
angelica leaves

Split the sponge cakes and spread the halves with jam. Arrange in a glass dish, pour over the sherry and soak for 30 minutes. Sprinkle ratafia biscuits over soaked sponge cakes. Pour custard on top to coat, and leave until cold. Whisk cream until thick, fold in sugar. Spread cream evenly over top of custard. Decorate with almonds, cherries and angelica.

STRAWBERRY MOUSSE

Serves 4–6

METRIC/IMPERIAL

450 g/1 lb fresh strawberries
juice of ½ lemon
75 g/3 oz castor sugar
15 g/½ oz powdered gelatine
4 tablespoons hot water

300 ml/½ pint single cream or
    evaporated milk
2 egg whites
strawberry colouring (optional)

Hull the strawberries; reserve a few for decoration. Sprinkle remainder with the lemon juice and sugar to taste. Leave to stand for a short while, then rub through a sieve to form a purée. Dissolve the gelatine in the water over a gentle heat, stir into the purée. Add the cream or evaporated milk and stir until well blended. Whisk the egg whites until stiff, then carefully fold into mixture. Add a few drops of strawberry colouring if liked. Pour into a glass serving bowl. Leave to set in a cool place for several hours. Decorate with remaining strawberries.

HALLOWE'EN PUMPKIN PIE

Cooking time 35–40 minutes
Oven temperature Moderately hot
190°C, 375°F, Gas Mark 5
Serves 4–6

METRIC/IMPERIAL

350 g/12 oz short crust pastry
  (see page 69)
milk and castor sugar for topping
for filling
900 ml/1½ pints strained, cooked
  pumpkin

1 kg/2 lb cooking apples, peeled,
  cored and sliced
225 g/8 oz sugar
½ teaspoon ground cinnamon
½ teaspoon grated nutmeg
½ teaspoon ground ginger
¼ teaspoon ground cloves

Combine the pumpkin, apples, sugar, cinnamon, nutmeg, ginger and
cloves. Mix well and turn into a large pie dish. Cover with the
rolled-out pastry, flute the edges and decorate the top with pastry
leaves. Brush with milk and bake in a moderately hot oven for 35–40
minutes, or until apples are tender and pastry is golden.

Serve hot, sprinkled with castor sugar.

Drinks

One important thing to remember about drinks: when cold they should be very cold and when hot, they should be really hot, not just lukewarm.

Summer drinks and wine cups are easily chilled in the refrigerator or with ice cubes, but care is needed in heating mulled drinks and wine cups. The liquid containing spirits or wine should never be boiled, but heated slowly to just below boiling point.

Some wine merchants will now hire you complete wine mulling equipment so that your brew stays at the correct temperature. The old way was to warm it by inserting a red-hot poker.

Punch bowls can also be hired. However, a large earthenware jug will do just as well, or your biggest mixing bowl, which can be beautified with fresh foliage from the garden.

If you're using delicate glasses for hot drinks, then warm them through first or place a silver spoon in each glass before filling it to prevent cracking.

To frost glasses for wine cups

Lightly beat the white of an egg, dip the rims of the glasses in the egg and then in castor sugar. Set aside to dry and harden before use.

Cold Drinks

ORANGE COOLER

Serves 3

METRIC/IMPERIAL

450 ml/¾ pint milk	whipped double cream
150 ml/¼ pint orange squash	crystallised orange slices

Whisk the milk and orange squash together. Pour into glasses and top with whipped cream. Garnish with crystallised orange slices.

LEMONADE

Serves 6

METRIC/IMPERIAL

3 lemons

175–225 g/6–8 oz sugar

900 ml/1½ pints boiling water

ice

twist of lemon

Wipe the lemons and finely grate the rind. Place the rind in a bowl with sugar to taste and pour in the boiling water. Cover and stand until cool. Add the juice of the lemons and strain into a jug. Place ice and a twist of lemon in each glass and top up with lemonade.

BLACKCURRANT WHIP

Serves 3

METRIC/IMPERIAL

4 tablespoons sieved
blackcurrant jam *or*

150 ml/¼ pint fresh blackcurrant
purée

600 ml/1 pint milk

sugar to taste

brickette or small carton ice
cream

Whisk the blackcurrant jam or purée into the milk. Add the sugar and chill well. Pour into glasses and top with ice cream.

HONEY AND ALMOND SHAKE

Serves 3

METRIC/IMPERIAL

1 tablespoon clear honey

25 g/1 oz ground almonds

600 ml/1 pint milk

little green colouring (optional)

1 egg white

whipped double cream

chopped almonds

Whisk the honey and ground almonds into the milk. Add colouring. Whisk the egg white stiffly and fold into the mixture. Pour into glasses and top with the whipped cream and chopped almonds.

ICED COFFEE

Serves 3

METRIC/IMPERIAL

50 g/2 oz sugar
150 ml/¼ pint hot strong coffee
450 ml/¾ pint milk

brickette or small carton ice
cream
grated chocolate

Dissolve the sugar in the coffee. Add the milk and chill well. Pour into glasses and top with ice cream and sprinkle with grated chocolate.

APPLE AND ORANGE REFRESHER

Serves 4–5

METRIC/IMPERIAL

450 g/1 lb dessert apples, peeled,
  cored and chopped
juice of 1 lemon and water to
  make 200 ml/⅓ pint

25 g/1 oz sugar
juice of 3 oranges
for garnish
orange wedges

Simmer the apples in the lemon juice and water and sugar until just tender. Blend in a liquidiser until smooth, mix with orange juice. Chill thoroughly. Serve in tall, stemmed glasses, place an orange wedge on the side of each glass.

INDIAN SUMMER CIDER

Serves 4

METRIC/IMPERIAL

4 teaspoons castor sugar
300 ml/½ pint freshly made
  medium strength Indian tea

300 ml/½ pint cider
crushed ice
4 slices lemon

Add the sugar to the tea, stir until dissolved. Combine with the cider. Chill. Cover the base of each glass with crushed ice. Fill with the tea and cider mixture. Add a slice of lemon to each.

WINE COBBLER

Serves about 14

METRIC/IMPERIAL

few ice cubes
1 lemon, thinly sliced
few sprigs mint
few maraschino cherries

1 bottle white wine
4 tablespoons lime juice
600 ml/1 pint soda water

Put the ice cubes, lemon slices, mint sprigs and cherries in the bottom of a large glass bowl or punch bowl. Pour the wine over and add lime juice and soda water.

POMAGNE JULEP

Serves 1

METRIC/IMPERIAL

1 teaspoon sugar
1 sprig fresh mint
1 teaspoon lemon juice

3 ice cubes or crushed ice
1 slice lemon
Pomagne cider

Put the sugar, mint and lemon juice into a tall tumbler. Stir briskly to bruise the mint and extract the flavour. Add the ice. Stand the lemon slice on rim of the glass. Two-thirds fill with Pomagne cider. Stir and serve.

Hot Drinks

CHOCOLATE NOG

Serves 3

METRIC/IMPERIAL

2 eggs whites
2 teaspoons brown sugar
2 teaspoons chocolate powder

600 ml/1 pint milk
1 tablespoon brandy (optional)

Whisk the egg whites. Add sugar and chocolate powder. Heat the milk and fold in egg white mixture. Add the brandy and serve immediately.

EGG FLIP

Serves 1–2

METRIC/IMPERIAL

1 egg
1 teaspoon sugar

2 teaspoons sherry
300 ml/½ pint milk

Beat together the egg, sugar and sherry. Warm the milk and add it to
the mixture. Heat slowly but do not allow to boil.

BLACKCURRANT SOOTHER

Serves 1

METRIC/IMPERIAL

2–3 tablespoons blackcurrant
  syrup
juice of ½ lemon

1 teaspoon clear honey
½ slice lemon

Measure the blackcurrant syrup into a heatproof glass beaker. Add
the lemon juice and honey. Fill up with boiling water. Float the
lemon slice on top.

TREACLE POSSET

Serves 3

METRIC/IMPERIAL

600 ml/1 pint milk
2 tablespoons black treacle

3 teaspoons double cream
a little powdered cinnamon

Heat the milk and dissolve the treacle in it. When sufficiently hot,
pour into cups and float double cream on top. Sprinkle with cinnamon.

Note Cream will float if it is poured over the back of a cold spoon
held so that its tip almost touches the surface of the liquid.

HOT TODDY

Serves 1

METRIC/IMPERIAL

1 tablespoon clear honey   1 tablespoon whisky
juice of ½ lemon   1 slice lemon

Put the honey, lemon juice and whisky into a heatproof tumbler or beaker. Fill up with boiling water and stir well. Float a slice of lemon on top. Serve very hot as a nightcap.

'SWEET DREAMS' NIGHTCAP

Serves 1

METRIC/IMPERIAL

300 ml/½ pint warm milk   2 teaspoons rum
2 teaspoons clear honey

Heat the milk and honey until almost boiling. Pour into a warmed glass. Stir in the rum. Drink at once.

CIDER HONEY PUNCH

Serves about 16

METRIC/IMPERIAL

2 flagons cider   2 good pinches ground ginger
4 tablespoons thick honey   1 lemon, sliced
1 teaspoon powdered cinnamon   *to serve*
6 cloves   cinnamon sticks
good pinch nutmeg   lemon slices

Heat all ingredients together slowly, except for the decoration, until hot and nearly boiling. Do not bring to the boil, but stir, cover and leave to infuse for 15 minutes. Strain out the cloves and lemon slices and reheat gently. Pour into a warmed punch bowl or jug, and serve in glasses with handles for easy holding.

To serve

Place a cinnamon stick and piece of lemon in each glass.

GAELIC COFFEE

Serves 1

METRIC/IMPERIAL

2 lumps sugar
3 tablespoons Irish whiskey

hot black coffee
lightly whipped cream

Warm a large glass for each guest. Place sugar in the glass. Pour in the whiskey. Add very hot coffee and stir. Hold a teaspoon just above the level of the liquid. Pour in the cream over the spoon so that it floats on top. The true flavour is obtained by drinking the hot coffee and whiskey through the cream.

MULLED WINE

Serves 6–8

METRIC/IMPERIAL

1 bottle inexpensive red wine
3 tablespoons clear honey
good pinch cinnamon
1 orange studded with cloves

150–300 ml/¼–½ pint boiling water
3–4 tablespoons brandy

Gently heat together the wine, honey, cinnamon and the orange. Stir well and do not allow to boil. Add boiling water and pour into punch bowl or large jug. Just before serving stir in brandy.

BUTTERED RUM

Serves 1

METRIC/IMPERIAL

1 teaspoon castor sugar
75 ml/4 tablespoons boiling water

75 ml/4 tablespoons rum
pat butter
grated nutmeg

Heat a tumbler or china mug, and put in the sugar. Add the water, rum and butter and stir. Sprinkle with grated nutmeg and serve at once.

Index